Coffee and Conflict in Colombia

PETER LANG
PROMPT

PETER LANG
New York • Bern • Berlin
Brussels • Vienna • Oxford • Warsaw

Dylan Scudder

Coffee and Conflict in Colombia

Part of the Pentalemma Series on Managing Global Dilemmas

PETER LANG
New York • Bern • Berlin
Brussels • Vienna • Oxford • Warsaw

Library of Congress Cataloging-in-Publication Data

Names: Scudder, Dylan, author.
Title: Coffee and conflict in Colombia: part of the Pentalemma series
on managing global dilemmas / Dylan Scudder.
Description: New York: Peter Lang, 2020.
Includes bibliographical references.
Identifiers: LCCN 2019041664 | ISBN 978-1-4331-7568-8 (hardback: alk. paper)
ISBN 978-1-4331-7565-7 (ebook pdf)
ISBN 978-1-4331-7566-4 (epub) | ISBN 978-1-4331-7567-1 (mobi)
Subjects: LCSH: Coffee industry—Management—Colombia—Case studies. |
Coffee growers—Colombia—Case studies. | Industrial
relations—Columbia—Case studies. | Conflict management—
Colombia—Case studies.
Classification: LCC HD9199.C62 S38 | DDC 338.1/737309861—dc23
LC record available at https://lccn.loc.gov/2019041664
DOI 10.3726/b16468

Bibliographic information published by **Die Deutsche Nationalbibliothek**.
Die Deutsche Nationalbibliothek lists this publication in the "Deutsche
Nationalbibliografie"; detailed bibliographic data are available
on the Internet at http://dnb.d-nb.de/.

This publication has been peer reviewed and meets
the highest quality standards for content and production.

The paper in this book meets the guidelines for permanence and durability
of the Committee on Production Guidelines for Book Longevity
of the Council of Library Resources.

Printed in the United States of America

Understanding a question is half an answer.

—Socrates

Contents

Figures

Preface

Coffee and Conflict in Colombia provides readers with a hands-on approach to dealing with the complexities unique to international management. The book draws strategically on this complexity to help readers cultivate greater critical thinking. It goes beyond the usual static business decisions related to setting the right price or memorizing truisms of management, choosing instead dynamic real-world cases that require detailed deliberation and creative problem-solving. While the book has been fictionalized, it draws on firsthand fieldwork and rigorous research on actual business cases with many characteristics that readers will recognize.

Each of the three chapters in the book starts out with a brief background of the context and the company, and then confronts the reader with a formidable and escalating challenge to work through. The scenarios include a high degree of complexity that companies often face in fragile environments that are unusually uncertain, whether in developing or industrialized countries.

With a focus on cross-sector collaboration, and managing the tensions between financial, social and environmental priorities, the trilogy helps readers learn how to develop creative solutions to seemingly insurmountable dilemmas. The book contributes in this way to management skills as well as to the knowledge needed to resolve issues in economic development, peace and conflict studies, political science, international relations and related fields.

Although the topics deal with high levels of complexity, they are written in an engaging and accessible way for current and future managers interested in stakeholder management, business in developing countries, Corporate Social Responsibility (CSR), sustainable business, international entrepreneurship, strategic leadership and global business issues.

Coffee and Conflict in Colombia is written as a trilogy to let readers experience how a business challenge evolves over three distinct phases in one location. This design enables readers to "stack" their learning from one part of the book to another. As business issues take on an increasingly global character, the material is organized to help the next generation of business leaders prepare for a wide range of scenarios in uniquely challenging environments.

Acknowledgments

It was Johan Galtung, "Johan" as he preferred, who introduced me to conflict theory as a way of applying creative thinking to seemingly impossible problems, and as a way of making work and life more meaningful. Johan recommended me to an MA program in peace and conflict studies in 1996, which I enrolled in the following year. For the next four years, I traveled extensively with him to mediation interventions, lectures and workshops in Okinawa and across Europe. Johan offered me a position in his NGO, Transcend, and advised me on my master's thesis that explored the Transcend method of conflict transformation. During this time, he also arranged for me to do an internship at the United Nations (UN) in Geneva, which opened for me a rewarding career path at the UN and later in business and academia. Those first years with Johan were some of the most intense, educational and adventurous ones of my life. Each day was filled with hard work, friendship and undoubtedly more than our fair share of humor.

Ian Green was Chief of the United Nations Training Section in Geneva when he hired me as a training coordinator. Ian generously gave me the space to experiment and discover how to create productive learning environments. Though this proved quite costly for him at times, he always went out of his way to make sure I had everything I needed to grow professionally. I can do the work I do today only because of the opportunities I was given in that first stage of my career.

I want to thank Jane Nelson, both for the encouragement she provided me through her book, The Business of Peace, and especially for the personal guidance she gave me. Jane invited me to her office at Harvard University, where she shared with me inspiring insights into the field of business in areas at risk. Much of what I learned from her writings has illuminated for me how ethical decision-making impacts on firm value.

Kiyoshi Amemiya, the inventor of the now-famous demining equipment that transforms minefields into orchards, gave me a once-in-a-lifetime chance to work with him and his team of engineers on a mine-clearing project in Colombia. He provided me with an insider's perspective—even letting me test-drive the mine-clearing equipment to better understand some of the operator's challenges first-hand. The onsite experience helped me appreciate the complexity of working for peace in a way that is also financially sustainable.

In the very volatile days following the Great East Japan Earthquake, it was Ray Bremner OBE, then CEO of Unilever Japan, who offered me a seat at the table where he and other members of the crisis response team would meet to review and plan. This life-changing experience gave me a chance to see some of the leadership behind Unilever's promise of Doing Well by Doing Good in the extreme conditions of disaster relief. This book is very much an attempt to let the reader sit at that same table and join in the decision-making.

Finally, I owe a particular debt of gratitude to my editor and friend, David Hulme. David was helpfully relentless in getting me to think and write more clearly. Visiting David and Satoko for hikes and in-depth discussions at their home in the mountains on the outskirts of Tokyo provided me with the extra push I needed at critical moments along the way.

DYLAN SCUDDER
Tokyo
August 2019

Introduction

This book aims to help business leaders of today and tomorrow learn how to stay profitable in an increasingly volatile world. Coffee and Conflict in Colombia provides an immersive reading experience based on the real-world case of a global company with operations under a constant threat of escalating armed conflict. The central challenge is to reconcile the competing demands of diverse stakeholders: immediate and long-term profitability, social concerns and environmental priorities. The book is grounded in the insight that such issues are always interdependent. As such, companies that ignore their stakeholders put their own future viability at risk.

This is easy to say, but much more difficult to realize. Following the PDCA model made popular by W. Edward Deming and refined in Japan, the book is organized around the four phases of Planning, Doing, Checking and finally, Acting. Within this framework, readers develop competencies by working through business challenges that they prepare for, engage in, reflect on and then draw lessons from that can be applied to the next challenges they encounter. Readers work as managers at Pentalemma Inc., a major risk advisory which has several large multinationals in its client base. Coffee and Conflict in Colombia is part of a series of books on the theme of global dilemmas, each covering a different location and linked to a specific industry facing its own unique set of challenges. Each book is written as a trilogy with three distinct phases within each volume.

The main question is how to select an optimum business strategy from several that emerge during the session. Readers receive a series of reports and press releases, which generate a realistic working environment and expose them to modern business tools. Parallel to this, they are informed by various advisors, such as business mentors or problem-solving specialists. The experience of reading the book is similar to the experience of managing other urgent problems at work, namely, through a flurry of emails and discussions. Immediately after preparing for the upcoming scenario, it's down to business. Rather than the traditional outdoor adventure, classroom lecture or hi-tech animation, readers are embedded in a corporate team and focused on a complex issue that must be solved without delay.

Learning is optimized by immersing readers in high-impact business challenges through intense but entirely plausible scenarios. These might be set anywhere in the world—from Colombia to the Philippines. What they have in common is the struggle of making critical decisions in the face of uncertainty. Readers must find practical solutions within quickly changing, high-risk situations. By the end of each chapter, readers will have chosen the plan they think their client company should adopt. The outcome, in the form of client feedback, company results and broader social reaction, will be shared with them through review material that describes plausible outcomes to the decisions they made. Finally, they are provided with several pages in the back of the book where they can make notes of their progress and create an action plan for further development.

In short, the book emphasizes risk awareness and mitigation by helping current and future managers understand that failing to consider the potential consequences of their everyday decisions exposes them and their stakeholders to unnecessary risk.

Chapter One

Organizational Development

You are a manager at a company called Pentalemma Inc., which specializes in stakeholder management. The company took its name from the Greek *penta* (five) and *lemma* (assumption), the forgotten wisdom of identifying five solutions embedded within a problem and then choosing the best one.[1] Pentalemma's headquarters are near Geneva, Switzerland, with several hundred employees around the world. The most frequent problem that Pentalemma's clients have is that their stakeholders disagree with each other. Pentalemma's competitors are often unable to help their clients find solutions because they can only see two solutions. For them, all stakeholder problems are "dilemmas."

Pentalemma managers offer a better service because they can see five solutions to stakeholder problems. They find the client's most difficult problem, usually a disagreement between their stakeholders, and then create five options for them to choose from. Clients try to choose the best "win-win" option for themselves and their stakeholders.

As a Pentalemma manager, you help your clients improve their business performance by working with them to resolve as many stakeholder dilemmas as possible. Pentalemma's clients are major companies with offices in many countries around the world. Some of these offices are in unstable or high-risk environments. Your current client is a national coffee consortium called Caffeine Supply (CS). CS is in the province of North Santander, a highland coffee growing region in the north-east of Colombia (see Figure 1.1 here below).

Coffee production remains one of the most important contributors to the Colombian economy. CS is also a major contributor to the Colombian economy. The company has a successful history in the sector, but recently the industry has faced a decline at home and competition from abroad. Meanwhile, Colombia has been struggling with security problems, though as this scenario opens, the situation in the North Santander area is relatively peaceful.

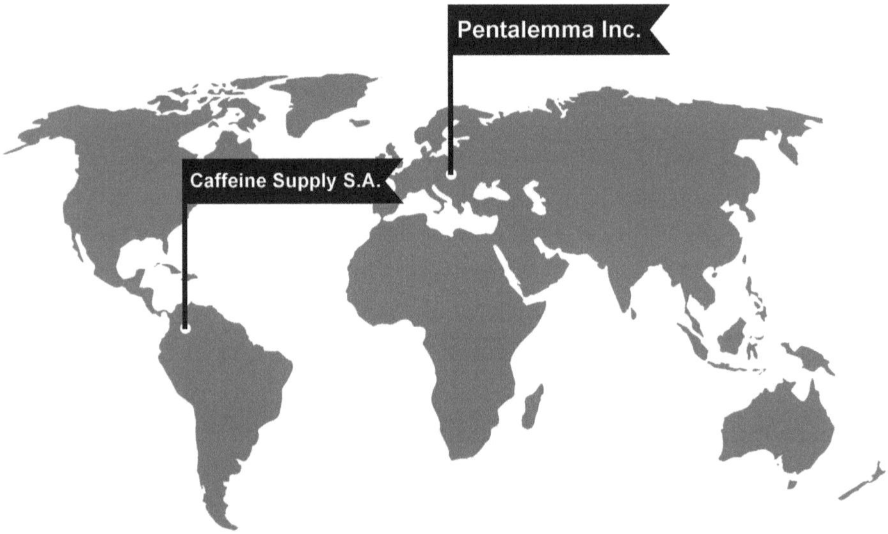

Figure 1.1: Locations of Pentalemma Inc. and Caffeine Supply.

Scenario Design

For many years, Colombia has been blighted by a four-way security struggle involving the (sometimes corrupt) security forces, the left-wing guerilla group Revolutionary Armed Forces of Colombia

(FARC), powerful narco-gangs and right-wing vigilante death squads. Thankfully many of these problems have now been brought under control, although by no means eliminated. The national economy is transforming and expanding. In many areas of the country, running a business brings the additional challenges of operating against this potentially explosive backdrop. The unfortunate fact is that many young people have to decide between working on farms or fighting for one of the military or paramilitary groups. Fighting is much more dangerous than farm work but may provide better pay for young villagers who need to support their families.

This scenario was designed to recreate some of that tension and, specifically, to explore the relationship between security and employment conditions.

Beyond the dynamics of security, politics and employment, a range of interconnected environmental issues further challenge Pentalemma consultants and CS managers. These take center stage in later scenarios, but their outlines are sketched in here. We learn that increasing rainfall (and subsequent explosion in insect-pest populations) is affecting production, particularly in the more marginal high-altitude locations. The solution seems to be insecticide spraying—which is subject to criticism from environmental groups.

One choice that CS, as a regional coffee consortium, must consider is to pay higher wages, but at the direct expense of long-term investment returns. Alternatively, it could accept the security risk associated with worker discontent and simply freeze wages. Other options are more nuanced, with the possibility of greater worker involvement in the marketing strategy, or a modest wage deal based on a no-strike agreement. The most successful choice is that to move toward profit sharing and Fair Trade certification (Fair Trade is a designation developed to help consumers support products that come from farms that have been certified to provide fair wages and safe working conditions). This is not as one-sided a deal as it might seem, as the key component is a measure of risk-sharing by all parties: the workforce would have a stake in the future of the organization.

Learning points, therefore, focus on the volatility of the security situation and how that reads straight across to the terms and conditions offered by major local employers. In turn, managers will appreciate that profit-sharing schemes can move beyond philanthropy into notions of a shared future.

In many respects, the Field Report that introduces the scenario is an upbeat one. We learn that a long-term improvement plan, entailing opening up new land to coffee production and replacing older coffee plants, is progressing on schedule. The immediate problem facing the regional coordinator for CS involves wages paid to farm laborers. International pricing is so tight that it seems any kind of wage increase will be extremely difficult for CS or its member farmers to afford. Yet the farmworkers have organized themselves into a trade union that has a highly capable individual to lead negotiations.

The straightforward approach to this situation is to view it in isolation, in terms of "pure" business economics. Importantly, managers are given several clues about linkages between employment conditions and overall security. Bread-line wages are likely to lead to increasing discontent and radicalization. In turn, this can play into the hands of rebel groups such as the notorious FARC. The security situation, too, is complex. CS also needs to be mindful of the role that right-wing vigilantes have played in Colombia's recent history.

Other problems and tensions have been woven into the narrative to provide greater challenge and authenticity. CS is about to launch a new up-market retail range, supported by an ambitious advertising campaign. The future of the industry hinges on its success. Can the trade union be brought in to the picture, so that they understand the criticality of this period, perhaps with promises about future profit-sharing? With environmental concerns such as the changing climate affecting yields, CS faces a multi-faceted risk landscape. Care will be needed in selecting a strategy that both safeguards the current growth plan and defuses a potentially explosive industrial relations dispute.

In your inbox is a report from Francisco Villa, the CS regional coordinator in North Santander.

Field Report

CAFFEINE SUPPLY INC.

From: Francisco Villa, Regional Coordinator, Norte de Santander
Subject: The Question of Wages

The overall situation for this month in the Norte de Santander coffee growing area remains positive. The plans for increasing production are well in hand and on schedule. We expect to have an additional 220 hectares under cultivation by the next harvest, exceeding our initial target of 180. Replanting of existing farms is also on track and will exceed the annual target of 10%. As you know, many of our plants are old and this has contributed to recent low yields. For the most part, the risks to production in this area are macro or external, and beyond our ability to influence. For example, the hygiene regulations going into effect next year will force many of the packing houses to invest in renovation.

Security along the Colombia/Venezuela border has stabilized with the improved relations between the two countries. This may also have contributed to the reduction in guerilla activity, which seems to be at an all-time low. There have been no reported attacks by the FARC over the past month. Thankfully, most of their coca production is well to the south of here, and there are few people who agree with their vision. The result is that more people are coming back to the farms. The benefit for us is that we currently have sufficient labor, but this may not last long as there are now attractive factory jobs in Cucuta.

Paramilitary pressure has eased, with farmers reporting little activity. As you know, I have direct contact with various representatives of farmworkers. They know they can communicate with us, and right now I am sure that most of them would prefer constructive dialog to unilateral agitation. Still, this could easily change.

My local problem right now is Los Trabajadores De Santander (TDS). You may have heard of this group. Membership among the coffee workers is now widespread (I would guess at over 50% in Norte Santander) and, in many ways, their ambitions are respectable. We do endeavor to care for our workforce, but we also have to operate in a global market. TDS seeks a minimum wage of $5 a day for coffee pickers and I have agreed to represent the growers on a Coffee Forum that they have established. I can see no harm in this. Meanwhile, we were able to pay only $3 last year. We also provide accommodation and food on many of the farms that we own or lease and manage directly. We also have a membership network of suppliers who either own or lease their plantations and pay workers out of their own pockets. There is no way these members can afford $5. But José Gravas, the local TDS Secretary, is a man I think I can do business with. He is also concerned, for example, about the use of children and pesticides. We will see.

Also of interest is the Campaign for Bird Friendly Coffee (CBC), a group that wrote to me last month from its new offices in Bogota. Basically, we have canopy cover for most of our production, so that we can honestly claim to be "bird-friendly" already. But there was a noisy demonstration in the capital a few weeks ago, so we should watch this one.

In conclusion, this is a rough period, but I believe it can be managed.
Francisco Villa
Regional Coordinator

You have been assigned to help CS managers to come to grips with the situation. In meetings with CS managers, you will explore the below topics:

1. The value of sharing profits—and risks—with the workforce.
2. The risk trade-off between long-term investment and the need to mitigate more immediate threats.
3. The links between local employment conditions, radicalization and security.

The many issues for discussion include working with trade unions; international price volatility; the local impact of climate change; marketing initiatives and Colombia's four-cornered security situation.

Questions to Consider

1. Is it realistic for a company to think it might reduce the risk of rebel activity by paying its workers more?
2. In a Fair Trade or profit-sharing model, is it the case that risks might be shared as well, or is this a myth?
3. Does the scenario point to ways of stepping beyond the tension between long-term investment and immediate risk mitigation?

Significant risks in Chapter One include:

Legal: To adhere to the hygiene regulations that will be in effect next year, CS will need to invest in upgrading its facilities.

Economic: TDS is pushing for higher wages, with good reason, but agreeing to their demands would be extremely costly for CS.

Demographic: Labor shortage might be an issue for CS this year, due to the creation of new and more attractive factory jobs in Cucuta.

Social: CS's security is likely to be affected by the local rebel movement, and the rural poverty that fuels it.

Ethical: Right-wing paramilitary forces have been a positive influence in the area, but they have also been responsible for death-squad killings. It is important that CS's stance, in this case, remains ethically informed.

Option A—Wage Freeze

It is difficult to satisfy the coffee workers in this part of Colombia without jeopardizing the price structure for the rest of the country. The best future for them is to recognize that in this national struggle, they are actually on the same side as the producers who support them. A wage-freeze this year is probably the best they can expect under the circumstances.

However, they do enjoy some job security and, in many cases, food and housing. This is quite exceptional in rural Colombia.

It is true that to take a strong position such as this is likely to provoke some FARC activity in the region (business continuity consultancy Rapid Response International has used its own statistical probability software to calculate a 90% possibility of this happening). In spite of this, CS would earn a profit. The same can be said of right-wing vigilante activity. There is also a 90% probability that, if FARC begins to cause trouble, vigilante "death squads" will make a reappearance. Even if FARC remains dormant, however, the return of the death squads would remain a 30% possibility as a result of radical voices in the workforce. This is regrettable but, ultimately, not seen as a direct CS's problem. Managers can only hope for the best.

You are awaiting a detailed Colombia Country Profile from Connie Bernstein,[2] Pentalemma's main contact at Rapid Response Inc. (RRI).[3] RRI is one of the world's leading risk management consultancies and is Pentalemma's worldwide source of intelligence on local developments. Bernstein provides the below interim note.

> "We need to consider the possibility of strikes. In this volatile security situation, this would be extremely unwise. My research suggests that a wage freeze would create an 80% chance of a strike this year. CS would have to manage that if it happens. The costs would amount to some $5m.
>
> I would advise all parties not to change anything this year. When the coffee prices rise, the wage question could be discussed again. These will be difficult times, but it is not CS's responsibility to provide security in this area. That is clearly a government responsibility, but CS could support the authorities in that effort.
>
> What we can say from our forecasting is that profit in this sector will remain resilient: If there are no strikes and no security issues, profit would be around $40m this year. But if there is any violence by FARC or vigilantes, profits may be only half of that. If both FARC and vigilantes cause violence, profits could sink to only $10m. We also have to consider that a strike could occur at any time."
>
> In summary, a wage freeze is a serious business decision. It is based on the fact that security is not CS's primary concern, and that business can continue even in difficult times. The best approach is for everyone to roll up our sleeves and continue working.

Option B—Pay at Least $4/Day

CS should take action now before worker unrest escalates. The cost of increasing daily remuneration to around $4 can be offset by restructuring investment in the coffee bush replanting program.

CS Regional Coordinator Francisco Villa sends you a personal message expressing his support for this option, reading in part:

> "The National University of Colombia recently published a report on the living standards in the region. It explains very clearly that $3 a day will not support a family of two even if they receive government support for housing and food. FARC has already put this report on its website! Our government is seriously worried about such threats and radicalization of the workforce through the TDS. It seems that CS will need to pay at least $4 a day.
>
> The cost to production and profitability in adopting this approach can easily be calculated. It is difficult to anticipate how the workers will respond to an offer of $4 a day. I think they are likely to negotiate for $5. If that happens, thinking about all the circumstances, we would probably have to accept. Of course, that would lead to further delays in replanting. If we paid $4 a day, we would most likely see production decline by 25%, but only for this first year. Shrewd rotation techniques might improve on this. If we had to pay $5 a day, there is a good chance of losing a bit more production. The operating factor here is that the more we pay, the fewer new plants we can put in, meaning that we become more dependent on the older and less productive plants."
>
> What is the impact of this on our profits? This is straightforward: by limiting lost production to 7 percent, profit would be around $20m; losing 15 percent reduces this to $15m; at 25 percent, $10m; and at 30 percent, we would have no profit at all. This is the cost situation. It becomes essential, therefore, to plan and manage the planting program intelligently. That is not an argument, however, for missing the opportunity to satisfy our workforce. It would be shortsighted to turn rural workers into rural insurgents.

Coffee and Conflict in Colombia

Having been presented with these two solutions, everyone on the Pentalemma and CS teams absorbs the RRI report, which contains a Colombia Country Profile and information on coffee and conflict.

From: Rapid Response Inc.
Subject: Country Profile for Colombia

Business Overview

Colombia is shaping up as a regional economic powerhouse. It is rich in natural resources, especially oil and minerals. It has a relatively open and fast-developing economy coupled with a stable democratic government. Though the infrastructure is being improved, the transportation network is patchy. The security situation has improved dramatically, but there are still regular reports of violence and localized instability.

Rapid Response Risk Assessment: Colombia at a Glance

Economy

GDP	$500 billion
Growth	4.3%
Inflation	3.2%
Unemployment	10.3%
Credit rating	Baa
Currency	1,900 Colombian Pesos = US$1

People

Form of government	Presidential democracy.
Ethnicity	50% Mestizo, 37% European, 9.5% African and 3.5% Amerindian.
Religion	Catholic 80%, Protestant 13% and others 7%. No particular tensions; secular state
Population	47 million

Infrastructure

Internet	Good
Roads	Average
Rail	Poor
Power	Excellent
Others	Proposed road/rail link coast to coast.

Background

Geography	Hugely diverse: mountains, jungle and savannah.
History	Tribal people until the Spanish conquest in 1499. Independence, 1819 ("Gran Colombia"); and modern borders and state date from 1886.
Natural resources	Oil, coal, rubies, hydro-electric potential and ecological diversity.

Politics and Government

Despite many years of violence and a brief period of dictatorship, Colombia has a long history of democratic government. The main traditional political parties are the Liberal Party and the Conservative Party. The former has an anti-clerical outlook and a commitment to free-market economics with a limited role for government. The Conservatives have strong ties to the Catholic Church and believe in a more central role for government. In the past, guerilla groups with socialist values have held significant numbers of parliamentary seats.

More recently, however, party politics has been quite stable. The Liberal Party is far less popular than the Social Party of National Unity (PSUN). A new alignment on the left has led to the rise of the Alternative Democratic Pole. Crucially, the Green Party, founded in 2005, came second just a few years later in the presidential election but fared poorly in the Congressional vote. The PSUN is the largest party in both chambers, followed by the Conservatives and the Liberals.

The Constitution provides for a powerful presidency, supported by a bicameral Congress. The system is based on strong regional and local governments. The PSUN has held the presidency in recent years.

Human rights violations are on the decline; press and media are both free, and international relations in the region are relatively stable.

Economy and Business

Colombia is a low-regulation, free-market economy that welcomes international trade and investment. With a 4% growth rate over the past few years, the macroeconomy is healthy. Government expenditure accounts for some 28% of GDP and the current year budget deficit stands at only 0.5%. Debt is running at 40% of GDP.

The country still has a large agricultural sector, but the service industries represent the heart of the economy, accounting for 55% of GDP and nearly 70% of employment. Industry is also important, with textiles, chemicals and oil representing major growth areas.

The stock market in Bogota is highly regarded and in 2011 merged with the exchanges of both Chile and Peru to form MILA (Mercado Integrado Latinoamericano), commonly referred to as the Andean Exchange—within which it is clearly the senior partner.

The trade union movement was a hotbed for radicalism 30 years ago, but is much weaker today. Only 4% of the workforce in the country is unionized. Industrial relations are generally smooth, with a workforce that is young and cheap. Unemployment stands at about 10%.

Corruption within business and government is low by Latin American standards, and at much lower levels than it once was; however, it remains a problem and business will need to be aware of this. Government accounts and statistics are mostly reliable.

Natural Resources

Colombia is a lucky country in terms of its natural heritage. There are large known deposits of oil, rubies, gold and coal. The country has huge potential for hydro-electric power projects. Much of the farmland is suitable for cash crops, not only coca but also coffee, for which the country is famous.

Brazil and Colombia are the largest producers of arabica coffee in the world, and this is a major factor in their current price war. Leaders from the two countries met last month at the headquarters of Colombia's agriculture ministry in Bogota to explore a sustainable way forward. Representatives from the Colombian Coffee Growers Federation and the Brazil Specialty Coffee Association told the press, "Coffee prices in both countries have plummeted so low that they are now even below production costs, which harms both countries and coffee-producing regions around the world. This degree of uncertainty will soon be felt not only by growers but by consumers too."

Over the past 15 years, the price for coffee has consistently hovered over US1$/lb, but has now dropped below 85 cents. This is far below what the millions of coffee farmers around the world would need to cover the cost of production.

Besides agriculture, there is also some scope for environmental tourism and related business as Colombia's biodiversity is world-renowned. This may bring commercial tensions. Green politics have a growing base of support; the Bird Friendly Coffee campaign is only one example of a sophisticated and well-funded pressure group now operating in the country.

Security

Security problems have burdened Colombian society for decades; only in recent years has the government been able to get the situation under control. The main opposition guerilla group is FARC (Revolutionary Armed Forces of Colombia), which still controls about 5% of the countryside. Though outwardly Marxist, FARC's real interests are in narcotics trafficking. The country also has problems with conventional organized crime syndicates that have clashed with security forces. Finally, the country has a history of right-wing death squads, sometimes working in collusion with the army and the police. They have mostly targeted FARC and trade union activists. Security in Colombia is therefore complex, but better than it once was. For businesses, the risk will depend on where they operate and in which sector. Commerce is safe in most places, but not all.

Rapid Response International consultants are experts in each region of the world. For research into specific risks, situations or crisis areas, the best decision a modern business can make is to ask for a special RRI Report. Our reports are always up-to-date and are written specifically for your business requirements.

Expanding the Menu of Options

You arrange several interviews with CS to bring in new perspectives and insights. You remind your counterparts that the objective is to build a strategy to satisfy CS's interests, improve the situation for farm-workers and to protect local wildlife. Using the Pentalemma method, you reconfirm the main problem. Who are CS's stakeholders? Does CS have cooperative relations with them? What are the most important issues that need to be resolved? After several intense rounds of discussion, you identify three groups who offer new options; C, D and E:

Option C—Engage with the TDS

"I can understand the concerns of our farmers in North Santander," says the representative of the Option C group. "We cannot ignore them and just hope that the unions will go away. We know that a number of national initiatives are underway, which may help us in due course. The new Colombian Coffee advertising campaign in Europe and the Far East begins in just over a month from now. This aims to promote our coffee in a new way to justify a higher price (the 'Life's Little Luxuries' range)."

The independent marketing consultants advise that the launch has a 30% chance of immediate success, a 30% chance of failing, or a 40% chance of a "slow burn"—i.e., no obvious results this year. If that happens, CS's coffee workers would certainly lose patience with this initiative.

> "Why not involve the TDS (Los Trabajadores De Santander) people in this by explaining the strategy to them? Mr. Gravas seems to be the kind of man who might respond to this. I would be happy to have an honest exchange with him in which CS agrees to review the situation in six months. He could influence the workers and help them recognize that we are all in this together.
>
> The risk is that the workers could strike, which is something Mr. Gravas has already mentioned. This would be less likely if the 'Life's Little Luxuries' campaign is successful—it would reduce the risk to an estimated 20% chance. But if the result turned out to be a slow burner, Mr. Gravas has been saying that workers' frustration would build quickly, making the likelihood of strike 90%. A failed product could also trigger a strike, a probability we estimate at 70%.
>
> The accountants in Bogota have looked at the impact of this high-risk strategy on this year's profits. If the new line takes off, CS could expect to net \$30m this year. If it flops, that would drop to \$15m. An indecisive 'slow-burn'

launch would generate $20m. But under any of these scenarios, a strike would cost CS about $10m over the year.

Despite these risks, it would seem foolish not to use this major marketing initiative as an opportunity to defuse this potentially damaging industrial relations problem."

Option D—Initiate Give and Take

A spokesperson for Option D confides the following:

"This is an extremely difficult situation, but we need to engage in some hard bargaining with TDS and the workforce. We need to be careful about this issue of radicalization. Local sources tell me that even with a good deal in place, there is a 50–50 bet that this will get worse over the year; that would in turn impact upon the security situation, as the RRI report makes clear. A more radicalized workforce would almost certainly lead to a worsening security situation, and I estimate that, under such circumstances, we would only have a 10% chance of stabilizing or improving matters. Without further radicalization, though, that chance would go up to 60%. I understand that a wage of $3.50 is sustainable at current prices, but I also recognize that this remains a minimal payment. Employers will need to improve the package in other ways: for example, a guarantee of year-round employment, accommodation and food. We are told that the new brand may let us raise the price for small wholesale before the end of the year. If so, CS should share some of this when it occurs. The workers could offer a no-strike deal and flexibility on overtime. Assuming the security situation remains stable, we could confidently predict profits of about $50m for the year ahead. If we got the strikes and demonstrations that we've had in the past, you could lop $5m off that. Furthermore, our work on security costs and insurance suggests that a worsened security situation would add $25m to CS's costs for the year.

In short, this situation is very tricky for CS; but some 'give and take' on both sides is surely possible and would serve to improve the overall situation and safeguard profits."

Option E—Fairtrade Certification

"In the long term, CS needs to explore the fairtrade certification concept," one of the managers closest to Francisco Villa tells you. "The big buyers in Europe, in particular, will pay a premium for fair trade coffee. The challenge,

> in this case, will be to undertake the difficult and lengthy process of application jointly with the TDS union. That way, the TDS people would feel invested in the success of the initiative from the beginning. At the same time, a profit-sharing scheme could be designed for the workers on each farm. The UN Trade Attaché, Mr. Samaras, would be a reliable advisor on these matters. This way, the future of the workers could be supported by the farms they work on."

The manager also refers to successful schemes on large farms in Honduras, where workers receive a plot of land to till for themselves. Many earn a valuable supplementary income with crops such as mange-tout peas or French beans. Some simply use the land for their own consumption.

"These are just ideas based on the notion of ensuring that the workers feel they are part of the operation and that they have a stake in its future," he explains. "The big payoff here," he adds, "could be a change in the attitude of the workers."

He cites an RRI study showing that the chances of further radicalization would be reduced to as little as 10% if a long-term deal of this sort were to be struck. On the heels of a non-radicalized workforce would come an 80% chance of stable or even improved security—whereas if the workers' attitudes hardened, the study predicts a 60% chance of weakened security.

The reward for success, according to the study, would be increased production, productivity and profitability for the long term. It projects profits of about $60m for the year following certification—if the security situation remains relatively stable. The figure drops to $45m or only $30m with worker radicalization.

It seems that pursuing Fair Trade certification would carry certain risks and costs, but it remains a possibility worth examining.

Initial Impact on Reputation

Based on initial feedback, CS attempts to analyze the potential impact of the various options on its reputation. You help them to organize a two-part workshop in which participants are asked to imagine the media reports resulting from each of the five possible choices. In the morning part-one session, they write these "media reports" for discussion.

Option A—Wage freeze—Coffee Workers Strike as FARC Resurfaces in Santander

The refusal of Caffeine Supply (CS) to offer a pay increase in the volatile North Santander province has triggered a walkout. Workers at seven large plantations refused to continue with planting and pruning operations on Tuesday, in a move organized by Los Trabajadores De Santander (TDS). By Friday, a silo belonging to one of the farms had been blown up in a guerilla attack widely attributed to the Revolutionary Armed Forces of Colombia (FARC). "You cannot isolate these two episodes," said José Gravas of TDS. "We oppose all violence, but there is no doubt that when people are desperate FARC will find it much easier to recruit around here."

Option B—Caffeine Supply Pays $4.00/Day in Landmark Deal

In a deal seen as out of step with price trends and the rest of the coffee industry, CS's Santander operation has agreed to pay its workers $4.00 a day for the forthcoming year. CS shares tumbled from $3.83 to $3.47 on the news, and there were angry scenes at the company's National Planning Committee in Bogota on Monday. Local CS chief Francisco Villa was unrepentant: "What we have done here is to secure a living wage for our workers, on whom we depend absolutely. We will recover the cost through our plantation management strategy." CS shareholders do not seem to share Villa's confidence.

Option C—Engage with the TDS—Union Urged to be Patient

TDS was asked for patience yesterday after a tense meeting with the CS management. CS is confident that its new products and marketing drive will push up overseas sales over the next six months. At that stage, it has promised a review of wages. "Our workers are starving now!" said José Gravas of TDS. It is not clear how long this shaky truce will last. Tensions are high in Santander, where paramilitary and guerrilla violence have blighted development for decades.

Option D—Initiate Give and Take—No-strike Deal for North Santander

It was smiles at last for TDS and CS representatives after a grueling seven-hour meeting to discuss the coffee crisis yesterday. The strike is off—for this year at least. And the coffee workers will get a small raise to $3.50. They will also get a guarantee of employment and the chance of more pay if CS's sales continue to grow. In an ominous development, one landowner, who refused to be named, said: "There will be violence if the Communists try to get any more money from the growers; enough is enough." Paramilitary activity has been a problem here in the past. But for now, this deal looks reasonably durable.

Option E—Certification—CS, Farmers and Workers Agree on Fair Trade Deal

It may take a year or more, but the CS regional operation in North Santander has decided to make a joint application for fair-trade status, supported by TDS. In the meantime, what has been regarded locally as a radical profit-sharing deal has been agreed, in a meeting chaired by mediator Kenny Raval. Mr. Raval was clear that the deal cuts both ways: "The workers have responsibilities here too. What profit-share does is give them a genuine stake, but that means sharing risk as well." TDS issued a statement that stressed the long-term nature of the deal. "What this means for us is a partnership, rather than the perennial arguments about wages. We hope that this will put us all on the same side." Commentators have underlined the broader importance of the deal for the security situation. An army source said that this was a bad day for FARC and the paramilitaries.

The workshop continues into the afternoon, with CS managers projecting their potential-outcome analyses further into the future.

Later Impact on Reputation—Media Reaction

Option A—Wage Freeze

With one or two local exceptions, there was barely any media reaction to the decision to freeze the wages of plantation workers this year. Nationally, the press has generally taken a sympathetic stance toward Caffeine Supply (CS). The national press also largely ignored the strikes. There has been plenty of coverage of FARC attacks and the re-appearance of death squads. With few exceptions, reports made no explicit linkage to the strikes.

Option B—Pay at Least $4/Day

The local leader of TDS, José Gravas, ensured considerable exposure for the $4-a-day coffee deal in Santander. It made the lead story on most of the national stations and was picked up for a feature by CNN. Editorially, most in the media see justice here, and the settlement will reflect well on CS.

Option C—Engage with the TDS

There has been no coverage to speak of concerning the wages situation in North Santander. The tacit agreement between TDS and CS not to promote the story explains this. Farmers and TDS have been keeping an eye on the "Life's Little Luxuries" campaign overseas. Steady success in growing sales volume at higher prices is generating much-needed optimism.

Option D—Initiate Give and Take

The no-strike deal came across as a bit of a lame story in most of the national media, only registering as a breakthrough on local TV. José Gravas of TDS gave an expansive interview to an early evening news show in which he demonstrated a mature grasp of the constraints facing the farmers. So locally, it played well. The message was that this was a clever deal from which all would benefit.

Option E—Fair Trade Certification

"Down on the Hacienda" ran initially as a piece by a stringer in one of the Colombian national dailies. It was picked up by Time magazine and given a three-page spread. The tone was entirely supportive, with lots of commentary about future development models. There were literally hundreds of spin-off stories across cable TV and the Internet. Locally, the initiative continues to garner extensive coverage, all of it positive. The Journal of Strategic Studies (London) has commissioned an article intended to examine the impact on security, speculating that all three of the "bad guys"—narco-criminals, FARC and the para-militaries—will lose support. This breakthrough deal secured a real PR coup.

At this point, let us fast-forward to consider five hypothetical sets of consequences according to assessments by CS itself.

General Impact on Firm Value

Option A—Wage Freeze

COMPANY REPUTATION: Freezing the wages in the North Santander area resulted in a strike by the region's workforce. It also caused the reappearance of FARC activity and vigilante death squads in the region. To say the company's reputation has suffered a hit in the past year would be an understatement. Workers are now despondent and more determined than ever to fight for a fair wage. This cost our company $2,500,000.

SALES: Due to the strike and guerilla activity, sales suffered more than they should have in the past year. Without workers to harvest the coffee beans, many crops were lost and uncultivated. Sales were down to $30,000,000.

RISK MANAGEMENT: Security costs have escalated due to increased violence. In addition, insurance premiums have soared, and farmers have resorted to costly agency staff in order to get vital work done. Risk management value has plummeted to negative $3,000,000.

SAVINGS IN SUPPLY COSTS: There was no saving in supply costs as our economies of scale were not achieved due to lost production. We violated many of the terms of contracts with our distributors and were unable to meet all of their needs. Therefore, there was no value added in supply cost savings.

STAFF MOTIVATION: Staff motivation is obviously low, and that's an understatement. The threat of death squads has many of the trade union members fearful for their lives. The atmosphere on many of the farms can be characterized as toxic—with goodwill virtually non-existent and productivity at an all-time low. All told, there was a negative $2,500,000 in cost associated with low staff motivation.

Option B—Pay at Least $4/Day

COMPANY REPUTATION: CS's offer of $4 per day in wages was not met happily, but it did prevent a strike from occurring in the region. Although strikes were avoided, reputation was damaged when CS had to acknowledge that the cost of the wage hike would be taken out of future investment in replanting to improve yields. Also, reports are flowing back to investors about the problems the company is facing in the region, resulting in a depressed stock price. The net value added is zero.

SALES: Production dipped even with the wage increase, but this was to be expected given the consequent inability to invest in replanting. This dip in production is not expected to continue in the long run. The net value added is $33,000,000.

RISK MANAGEMENT: CS was able to hold off a strike and prevent an uptick in FARC activity in the region. There is no evidence of TDS unionists gravitating to the FARC camp. Thankfully, there have been no reports of death squads. It seems that having a job, even with unsatisfactory (to them) wages is preferable to joining a violent terrorist group. The net value added was $2,500,000.

SAVINGS IN SUPPLY COSTS: Setting labor costs aside, both fuel and fertilizer prices fell slightly during the second half of the year. This offset some of the impact of the wage deal and allowed most farms to secure planned savings. All told, the net savings came in at $5,000,000.

STAFF MOTIVATION: The mood amongst the workforce has generally been buoyant, resulting in much-improved productivity and attendance. A difficult industrial relations issue has certainly been snuffed out here, at least for the current year. All told our net value added for staff motivation was $5,000,000.

Option C—Engage with the TDS—Await the Outcome of New Marketing Campaign

COMPANY REPUTATION: The Company's reputation was increased by moving its product upmarket. The "Life's Little Luxuries" advertising campaign was a success. We explained this to the TDS representative, who in turn conveyed our position to the TDS membership. This shielded the company from the negative publicity usually associated with a strike. The net value added is $4,000,000.

SALES: Sales were up as we had more hectares come online in the past year, alongside the advertising campaign. We have yet to address the issue of aging plants causing lower yields, and can expect production levels to remain fairly steady over the next few years. These factors led to a net value of sales at $45,000,000.

RISK MANAGEMENT: The discussions with the TDS effectively defused the strike risk for the current year, allowing for a secure environment around production processes and precluding any serious risk of FARC activity. Risk management costs were down commensurately. The net value for this compromise is $7,500,000.

SAVINGS IN SUPPLY COSTS: Production was up, and our supply chain targets were met. Logistically, we were able to leverage our immense purchasing power with local distributors, and ship increased volumes at lower rates per kilometer. The net value of these advantages was $5,500,000.

STAFF MOTIVATION: While it's still not the best, staff morale was steady as employees saw the campaign working and the price of the raw product surely expected to rise now. They know that this means they can revisit the issue of $5 per day wage in the near future once prices come back to normal ranges or even higher. The net value of this was $7,500,000.

Option D—Initiate Give and Take

COMPANY REPUTATION: At least a strike was avoided. Workers understood the benefits of what CS was offering and were motivated by its guarantees of year-round employment and profit-sharing if prices rise. This stability was also noted by our shareholders as the stock price held steady for the year. The net value of these actions was $9,000,000.

SALES: Sales were up with increased production in the region. Our 220 additional hectares were harvested, and we only saw slight drops in production from some of our older sites. Demand for our new luxury product is up around the world, which can only mean good things in the future for all parties involved. The net value of these production upswings is valued at $60,000,000.

RISK MANAGEMENT: No strike, no FARC activity in the region and higher production yields, everything CS hoped for under this option. That doesn't mean the elimination of all current and future risks, but it was encouraging that our actions minimized them for the time being. The net value added was $8,500,000.

SAVINGS IN SUPPLY COSTS: Supply costs were down as our logistics improved in several high-cost areas. We were able to purchase transportation at lower prices for our coffee, and that saved money on the bottom line. We expect that with even more increased future production, these savings will continue to grow. The initial estimates are a net value of $8,000,000.

STAFF MOTIVATION: This initiative was largely greeted as a fair settlement across the farms in the region, and some of the more heated elements in the TDS have lowered the volume. The result is a better working atmosphere, improved productivity and a positive attitude to the thorny overtime issue. Most farms report a harmonious situation with the workforce. Staff motivation is valued at $5,000,000 for the year.

Option E—Fair Trade Certification

COMPANY REPUTATION: The prospect of unrealistic demands for wage increases has all but been eliminated. By giving the workers and farmers a share of the profits and part of the land for their own farming and harvesting needs, CS has developed sustainable goodwill with the workers and TDS. This stability has contributed to an uptick of 10% in our share price. The net value of these actions is worth $12,500,000.

SALES: Sales were up more than expected as workers were motivated to harvest the highest yields possible, knowing that they had a stake in their success as well. We expect this trend to continue as we continue to expand our business and bring on more workers to develop more coffee crops for CS. The net value of these increases was $75,000,000.

RISK MANAGEMENT: The major risk in the region seems to be the FARC. However, with most of their activity confined to the south and with workers' motivation increased, it seems unlikely that they will gain a foothold in Santander in the foreseeable future. Outstanding concerns about the possibility of strike action or even sabotage seem unwarranted in the light of the new deal. Farmers have made direct savings in a number of areas as a result.

The net value added of mitigating the risks stands at $11,000,000.

SAVINGS IN SUPPLY COSTS: Increased production made our distributors happy as their sales rose and they offered discounts for our increased shipping needs. We expect these pro-rata savings to continue into the future based on the stability of the region and the contented workforce. Estimated net value is $11,000,000.

STAFF MOTIVATION: Workers are now motivated to produce the highest yields possible as they now have their own skin in the game. They are encouraged that as the prices rise, CS's bottom line won't be the only one that benefits. The continuing security improvements have added to worker and family wellbeing in the area, with many other family members taking advantage of the small plots of land made available to employees. CS in Santander has seen increased productivity and no walkouts over the past 12 months. The net value added is $4,500,000.

Reflecting on Chapter One

The Scenario in Context

This scenario introduced you and your consulting team to Colombia, a country with a difficult security situation but in other respects, a rather promising economic outlook. You were tasked with advising the local manager for Caffeine Supply in North Santander, whose chief concern was a wage claim from the workers on the coffee plantations. They had organized themselves into a trade union headed by a shrewd and determined negotiator.

The four-cornered security picture (security forces, left-wing guerilla group FARC, narco-gangs and right-wing death squads) was fundamental to this scenario, even though at the time the area enjoyed a period of relative peace. The obvious threat was from FARC, but your team and the CS managers also had to be mindful of the interests of the other three potentially dangerous groups.

An important factor in the formulation of various options concerned real or potential linkage between employment conditions in the area and the susceptibility of the local population to recruitment by criminal or rebel elements. The validity or otherwise of this proposition underlay most of the options and their consequences for Pentalemma and CS.

Dilemmas and Challenges

The central dilemma that managers should have spotted in this scenario was not that between the twin necessities of avoiding strike action and maintaining profitability, although this was an important consideration. The key tension was between profitability and security. CS needed to invest in its future in order to build the business and offset the competition from neighbors such as Brazil. Arguably more important, though, was the need to avoid creating circumstances that might jeopardize the fragile peace. A better understanding of the geometry of the security situation and the international competition was included in the "Country Profile" made available by Connie Bernstein.

Two other important tensions ran through the Field Report and accompanying Pentalemma Briefing. First, that between longer-term planning, represented by the targets for expansion and replanting, and the short term need to avoid a strike. Second, that between the nationally agreed plan and the local needs of coffee growers in North Santander.

There were no straightforward answers to these supplementary dilemmas, which in many ways cut across the central security risk. Instead, managers needed to engage carefully with the options available in order to determine which might best mitigate such risks while successfully addressing the central dilemma.

What may have occurred to you when discussing the various options with your colleagues was the shared interests between the coffee workers and the farm owners. Both sides needed a safe environment and an expanding coffee industry. This understanding offered a key to the various options presented and was one of the more useful means of assessing them.

Notes

1. The roots of the pentalemma perspective can be traced back as far as Aristotle and his square of opposition (Béziau & Payette, 2012). While it only defines four points of opposing propositions, a fifth mid-point of compromise between these can be inferred. The German philosopher, Johann Fichte, introduced the

thesis-antithesis-synthesis triad in his 1794/1795 publication, Foundations of the Science of Knowledge (Breazeale, 2013). This triad implies a process of reasoning that develops and then reconciles opposing views. Another German philosopher, Wilhelm Krug, made explicit mention of a pentalemma in 1827 in his dictionary of philosophical terms, defining it as a five-dimensional problem or "five-horned conclusion" (*ein fünf-gehörnter Schluß*). Between the 1950s to the 1970s, Norwegian sociologist and pioneer of peace and conflict studies, Johan Galtung, developed in his lectures and unpublished books a five-point model for analyzing social conflict. These were later published in the Encyclopedia of Violence, Peace and Conflict in 2008 (Kurtz, 2008). I had the opportunity to join many lectures and workshops over a period of several years in the 1990s in which Galtung would demonstrate how to analyze conflicts with the model. At a lecture he once gave in Germany in 1999, he drew the model on a flipchart while telling the students, "I don't understand why more people don't use this." I took note and began experimenting with it from that day. Galtung was the first person to publish analyses of social conflict from a five-point perspective, something he confirmed in a discussion I had with him about this at a conference in 2016 in Japan. In the management literature, Robert Blake and Jane Mouton (1964) developed a five-point model in their book *The Managerial Grid: The Key to Leadership Excellence*, differentiating between leadership styles in relation to a concern for people versus a concern for production. In 1981, Fisher, Ury and Patton then introduced a similar model for interest-based negotiation in their bestseller Getting to Yes. More recently, the model has also been used in the psychology and related coaching literature, as in Thomas Augspurger's 2008 book on constructive leadership. Different versions of the diagram are still used in game theory to depict Nash equilibrium or Pareto optimality. Drawing inspiration from these perspectives, especially Galtung's work on conflict theory, I apply the pentalemma model to the challenge of satisfying the competing needs of corporate stakeholders.

2. Connie Bernstein is a senior consultant at Rapid Response Inc., which she joined in 2011. Connie manages a small team of consultants who undertake detailed research on global "hotspots" and works with clients who need bespoke and intensive business continuity advice. She used every opportunity to keep her skills fresh by maintaining her own client portfolio and working on the frontline whenever she can. Much of her time these days, however, is devoted to building up the RRI Country Profile Service. This new service provides up-to-date summaries of countries around the world and what it means to do business in them.
3. Rapid Response Inc. (RRI) is one of the world's leading business continuity consultancies. The company provides advice on maintaining business in volatile and complex environments. Specialized in crisis management, RRI helps businesses secure their operations under extreme conditions such as natural or manmade disasters. Emphasizing foresight and preparation, the company believes that a well-prepared organization should be able to carry out its business in almost any

environment. The client base is diverse, including groups like Pentalemma that advise on broader areas of risk, multinationals, governments and individuals. RRI consultants have been recognized experts in their field since 1985. In the RRI reports, a "high" status does not mean simply "stop": it means stop, review and, where appropriate, proceed with caution. Between the extremes of "low" risk and "severe" environments, "guarded," "elevated" and "high" assessments may be regarded as transitional. These show when a country is moving significantly in one direction or another, and provide an overview of the security climate at a glance.

Further Reading

Béziau J.-Y., & Payette, G. (2012). *The square of opposition: a general framework for cognition*. Bern: Peter Lang.

Blake, R. R., & Mouton, J. S. (1964). *The managerial grid*. Houston, TX: Gulf Pubs.

Breazeale, D. (2013). *Thinking through the Wissenschaftslehre: themes from Fichte's early philosophy*. Oxford: Oxford University Press.

Fisher, R., & Ury, W. (1981). *Getting to yes*. Boston: Mifflin.

Galtung, J. (2008). *50 Years: 100 peace and conflict perspectives*. Oslo: Transcend University Press.

Krug, W. T. (1827). *Allgemeines Handwörterbuch der Philosophischen Wissenschaften*. Leipzig: F.A. Brockhaus.

Kurtz, L. (2008). *Encyclopedia of violence, peace, and conflict*. San Diego: Acad. Press.

Chapter Two

Action Research

Your assignment advising Caffeine Supply (CS), regarding the wages dispute between CS and its plantation workers in North Santander, was successful. Pentalemma has been retained to assist with negotiations related to a set of environmental issues. Now, although the threat of war and violence remains very real, the main current issue is that the continued expansion of CS plantations will depend on the use of organophosphate (OP) pesticides, the use of which will shortly be banned by the Colombian government. Besides, an environmental group has already threatened a product boycott.

You and your team can see that CS managers face a tricky set of choices as they attempt to assess the best means to address this pesticide problem. OP pesticides are cheap and indiscriminate: They kill at least as many "good" bugs as "bad" ones. Pricier alternatives are available in the form of species-specific products based on genetic modification. There is even a proposal to trial a predator-based solution with the participation of an Italian university.

Another element of the problem is that it is marginal land, which is very prone to invasion by the pests that destroy coffee plants. These are precisely the areas that need to be upgraded to keep the nationwide development plan on track. Furthermore, these areas are the most exposed to a recent upsurge in violence.

Running alongside this environmental and technical challenge is the Campaign for Bird Friendly Coffee (CBC). This group has been supportive of CS in the past but now seems entrenched in opposition to the question of OP pesticides. Meanwhile, the government in Bogota is pressing for more acreage because an economic downturn means factory closures, which in turn means workers returning to their villages looking for work in the agricultural sector. Managers need to tease out a solution that avoids a product boycott without throwing the company's vital expansion plans into jeopardy.

A series of meetings will explore:

1. Multi-faceted engagement with environmental groups, the media, academia and others.
2. The challenge of a rapidly changing technological and legislative environment.
3. Deal-making, between groups, seemingly implacably opposed to one another.

The many issues to be covered include economic downturns; modern pesticides; rural and urban migration; predator-based pest control; vigilantism; climate change and gain-share.

Scenario Design

The primary purpose of this scenario is to introduce consultants and managers to the controversy and challenge of modern agriculture—where technology meets the environment in the search for increased but sustainable production. Other factors remain in play, such as the continuing risk of violence and the general economic downturn in Colombia. These do have an influence on some of the options presented and in their outcomes, as expressed in the post scenario reports. A careful eye, therefore, needs to be kept on such background factors. Yet the key problem for managers here is the technical-environmental one centering on pesticides.

One of the important learning points in this situation concerns the dynamics of conflict resolution. However intractable an opposing group—CBC in this case—may seem, given goodwill on both sides there will usually be a way through. Management tools and techniques exist to help negotiators identify these.

Another key theme is a partnership, particularly with organizations from outside the world of business. It is difficult to exaggerate how important and widespread such relationships are in the modern corporate world. These players bring their own risks and challenges with them, and in this scenario, the teams have three such relationships to consider. There is the tempting proposal of a co-branding deal with CBC, the possibility of major sponsorship through a TV company and a related deal with an Italian university. Is it all good news or should managers approach these parties with caution?

Finally, there is the challenge of technology itself. Particularly when it has direct implications for the natural environment, this can be an extremely difficult aspect of risk management to address. It is common for competing and rapidly evolving technologies to present themselves at the same time. The business risks of getting it wrong typically include technical failure, environmental damage and public outcry. Nowhere is this more evident than in the modern farming sector.

Questions to Consider

1. What kind of risks should be assessed in partnering with the media, academia or environmental groups?
2. Is the search for common ground—sometimes involving hostile opinions and strong personalities—are there more objective resolutions methods that might be employed?

3. What factors should a farming business consider in assessing the three methods suggested in the scenario for combatting the red spider mite?

Significant risks in Chapter Two include:

Political: As violence remains an issue in the area, CS needs to remain diplomatic and avoid aggravating the ongoing tensions between the FARC and the TDS.

Environmental: Although pesticide use contributes to CS's bottom line in the short term, the natural environment in and around coffee growing areas is being polluted.

Economic: Given that the Colombian economy is officially in recession if CS were to simply accept the public's demands for no pesticide use, the effects on the company's finances would be disastrous.

Social: The recent economic recession in Colombia has exacerbated poverty and homelessness in rural areas. CS needs to consider the impact of its decisions on fragile communities already at risk.

Legal: The use of OP spraying will soon be considered unlawful in Colombia. Abiding by the law, however, means investing in alternative and particularly expensive types of pesticides, which would prevent CS from expanding its farmland as planned.

Your task, as always, is to assess the situation and help CS managers make good decisions. You will gather information from Pentalemma and from CS. You will contact experts to get their advice, and you will do your own research. Finally, you will report to the CEO of Pentalemma.

The second term of your deployment by Pentalemma kicks off with a report from CS Regional Coordinator Francisco Villa.

From: Francisco Villa, Regional Coordinator, Norte de Santander
Subject: The Question of Pest Control

Pentalemma Team,

I hope this update finds you well.

Annual figures now confirm that the Caffeine Supply Expansion Plan for Norte Santander was delivered to schedule last year. Total hectares under production are now in excess of 3500, the regional target. Our rotational target of replanting 10% a year was also achieved. I do have concerns, however, about the proposals from the recent National Council meeting (which I was unable to attend). Having reached these ambitious targets, we are now asked to secure an extra 200 hectares for the current season. There are some local factors that call this into question. Security is always a concern in this area and whilst FARC activity remains minimal (as far as I can ascertain), we have recently seen a spate of murders, appearing to target TDS leaders. It is true that TDS organized a two-day strike earlier in the year and there was a lot of anger among our members. I was personally criticized for my engagement with the TDS leadership. The $4 pay deal appears to have stabilized that situation, but my producers cannot continue to pay at that level unless the coffee price increases. I will, therefore, need some assurance on that. As you know, FARC was a big problem here not so long ago.

If recent events represent a resurgence of paramilitary violence, it cannot be good for the coffee industry. It is too soon to draw such a conclusion, and the State Governor is pushing the police hard on this issue.

More pressing right now is the question of pesticide control. Growers have again been plagued with red spider mite on the plants, resulting in a 60% loss of production on some of the smaller farms. The red spider mite infests the leaves of the coffee plant, puncturing the undersides in order to feed, until the leaf withers and dies. Spraying has proved effective—using the new insecticide secured through CS nationally—although not all of our producers can afford this. Some are still using the organophosphate (OP) sprays, which are attracting controversy.

Obviously, we cannot sell organic coffee if we are forced to spray, and going organic is not a realistic strategy for this region. The climate does seem to be changing here. We have more rain than we did 20 years ago, and this is encouraging the insects. More and more people regard coffee-growing as a marginal enterprise.

The problem is that the cheaper OP sprays are non-discriminating and, according to our critics, pose a hazard to the environment. Until very recently, we had a good rapport with CBC. As you know, our growing technique up here relies on canopy cover for the coffee plants, which is conducive to a diverse bird population. CBC is wary of the new spray, but absolutely opposes the use of OP sprays on coffee plants. The National Council is calling for more hectares, but I have to report that there is no way this can be achieved locally without more support: We need affordable sprays so that we can satisfy CBC.

To complicate matters, the State Governor is sending out mixed messages. I understand his support for tourism (and we have an important wildlife sanctuary), but coffee still represents over 50% of the local economy. Some lobbying at the national level would be of assistance.

We look forward to your thoughts on the best way forward.

Best regards,
Francisco Villa
Regional Coordinator

The Dilemma—Two Directions

A long day of intense discussion with CS managers and within the Pentalemma team boils down to two firm options, as summarized by the CS office.

Option A—Only Spray a Little OP

Evidence of the ill-effects of OP pesticides on bird populations is mixed, with no clear indication of species decline in North Santander. Furthermore, the extent of OP use in this area has declined and will continue to do so, with the government's ban due to come into force in three years. Pending that change, there is a case for selective OP use in the very marginal areas. This is an argument that can be won, especially as CS has a good track record of engagement with environmental groups and in responding to their concerns. The fact is that only some

25% of the coffee grown in this area would have been sprayed with OP, according to CS records. On that basis, it makes sense to complete the expansion plan now, advising farmers to use OP only where the red spider mite problem is at its worst. Those able to use light doses of the pricier GM products should do so. CS, with its sophisticated public relations operation, should be able to weather any protest on this basis. With this approach, we should hit its profit target for the year of $40m. But that assumes a stable security situation and no product boycott. Depending on whether security worsens or improves, profits could either drop to $20m or climb to $60m. Therefore, it is the security situation that is likely to have the greatest impact on profit this year, and this is something that we can do little to influence. There is a 50% chance of security in the region remaining stable, or a 20% chance of it improving. Or, of course, it could get worse.

We should also consider the product boycott threatened by CBC, in the light of their successful campaign against *High Blue* in Brazil. Irrespective of the security situation, there is an estimated 70% chance of CBC going ahead with a boycott. Instead, they might endeavor to lobby the government to bring in its ban on OP pesticides early—though this seems highly unlikely, perhaps with only a one-in-ten chance of succeeding.

We know that this year's spraying is a finite operation. We also know that GM pesticide prices will drop in the medium term and that without such an approach, CS's National Plan will not reach its target. Therefore, although CBC (and the security backdrop) poses serious risks, the argument for spraying seems solid.

Option B—Abandon OP Sprays

If CS is not very careful, it will make too many enemies. There is already a sensitive security situation in the region, and it is vital that we work with other parties in assuring zero contact with the paramilitary groups. We thought this problem was licked but if not, let's remind ourselves that we may well undermine the entire export program if there are any stories of "death squads" in the media. The other risk is environmental. It cannot be rational to insist on using OP chemicals when Colombia's own government has announced its abolition. This will simply have to be absorbed as a cost to CS at the national level—even while accepting that plantations at the very margins in North Santander have a particular problem. Note also the success of CBC against *High Blue* in Brazil. These people don't kid around. We will need to deliver some fairly blunt messaging in Bogota in order to ensure that the growers down in Santander receive a reality check.

However, there is a silver lining. If CS pulls back from some of its more marginal farmland because it decides not to use OP insecticides, it will not be operating in some of the more dangerous parts of the North Santander countryside. The farmers could well be safer. This will save on security and related costs. We estimate a 60% chance of a stable security situation for our farmers by using this approach, with a 30% chance of improvement. There is an outside chance of deterioration—as always in Colombia—but we are confident that this is no higher than 10%. We would hope that in reducing our hectarage in this way, the remaining farmland would be largely mite-free. There remains, however, a good chance of serious mite damage affecting our production. The chance of this occurring is about 80%. But with luck, we will be mite-free; there are no certainties in coffee growing.

CS's North Santander profits would, of course, be reduced on the back of this approach, but it would nonetheless provide us with a sustainable and uncontentious template for future years. If security remains stable, profits could reach $30m, or even $40m if it improves. Further deterioration would lower profits to $20m. Sadly, heavy mite damage would lower all profits by 50%.

Safety and security must be paramount concerns for CS. This approach is the only means we see for addressing that fundamental risk.

Action Research

You now have a general overview of the problems on the horizon and a hint of some solutions to the main issues. There are, however, more problems to come, and responses to consider. Looking for ways to make sense of this dynamic situation and develop a plan for the client, you email management advisor and "Master Facilitator" Fernando Rodriguez.

After reviewing the information that you shared with him, Rodriguez responds with a suggestion to apply a methodology called "action research." This is essentially a process of problem-solving that is similar to the four-step management cycle of planning, doing, checking and acting (PDCA).

> "This should be intuitive to you and your colleagues because you use a similar approach in your work," he explains (see Figure 2.1 here below). "In essence, this is a process of trial and error, but it is a systematic one. You have a goal, something you want to change or improve. The first step in the cycle is Planning, which means thinking about what needs to change in order to reach the goal you set out to achieve. Then you take some kind of action to achieve this goal and evaluate the results. It's not complicated. In the action research cycle, these are called Acting, and then Observing. What makes this process more systematic than basic common sense is the final step of Reflecting. This is where you ask yourself questions such as: "Why was the approach effective or ineffective?" or "What could be done to make it more effective next time around?" As you transfer your findings from one cycle to the next, your understanding increases in an upward-moving spiral until you either achieve or change your goal."

In a meeting to discuss Rodriguez's suggestion, a member of your team points out that using action research makes sense, but that it would be impossible to run these kinds of experiments with each of the options. She says what other members of the team are also thinking, namely, that CS expects Pentalemma to recommend a course of action, not to conduct a lengthy research project. "Frankly, we have neither the budget nor the time to be so scientific about this," she says.

After emailing your concerns to Rodriguez, he replies, "This is a common problem. It's not necessary to carry out time-consuming research projects. You can use this cycle to run hypothetical experiments,

First stage:	Plan—Act—Observe—Reflect
Next stages:	Plan—Act—Observe—Reflect
Final stage:	Plan—Act—Observe—Reflect

Figure 2.1: Repeating the P-A-O-R cycle stage by stage, Scudder (2019).

so-called thought experiments or forecasts. As Pentalemma always explores five different approaches to the problem at hand, you can use the collective experience in your team to imagine how each of the five approaches is likely to impact on firm value. It may be difficult to forecast the details, but you can use the collective experience in your team to imagine likely reactions in the media, for example. Doing this for each of the five options should give you a useful overview of the advantages and disadvantages of each option."

After some debate, your team agrees that Rodriguez's suggestion will help to evaluate the options and give CS a trustworthy recommendation. CS CEO Javier Rigas asks Rodriguez to work with the CS management team to develop three additional options. After some intense discussion and some healthy debate, they come up with new potential outcomes that one of the managers describes here below.

Option C—Engage with CBC and TDS

The situation in North Santander is at crisis point, and the rather sinister security backdrop makes it even more problematic. I wonder whether it might be possible to invite CBC to our meeting in Bogota or, perhaps, to the second half of it? I spoke to their Latin America Head, Christine Perez, yesterday and floated this idea. She was certainly open to negotiations. My purpose in taking this line is to bring the CBC people into the tent and appraise them of the entire context. The blunt truth is that we risk considerable bloodshed, unemployment and rural poverty if we don't get this right. CS, TDS and—I'm sure—CBC would want to avoid that and to have a grown-up discussion on that basis. None of these issues—pesticides, security and wages—can be dealt with in isolation. If I am to try to pick a way through them looking for compromise, I will need time. That would be my plea to Ms. Perez. Perhaps we could all agree on a cooling-off period coupled with creative thinking on all sides, and to come back to this once the main picking season is over.

Of course, such an approach leaves the overall security situation unaddressed. My sources in the government estimate a worrying 30% chance of it worsening through this year, which would have a major impact on our profitability. On a brighter note, I was told there was the same likelihood of an improved situation; or of course things could remain more or less as they are now. Beyond that, I suppose we should consider the possibility of talks with CBC breaking down entirely. Ironically, a worsened security situation would make this less likely, in that protesters would be less inclined to get involved in a hostile environment. My advisors estimate that under such circumstances, we would only face a 30% chance of the talks breaking down; otherwise, given CBS's record, I fear it would be 50%. Still, we should give it a try.

This is not an ideal backdrop for CS's profit outlook in North Santander. Should the talks keep going and security remain stable, net profits are estimated at $50m. They would even hit $60m if security actually improved, or drop to $20m if it worsened. I estimate the cost of a collapse in negotiations at $10m. In that case, CS will face increased security challenges and possibly some kind of boycott.

I trust that these extrapolations are helpful. Despite the very uncertain situation, I am sure that a strategy based on dialogue remains the only sensible course of action.

Option D—Settle Quickly—OP Phase-out

Fortunately, Ms. Perez proved more than willing to engage in discussion on the difficult issue of pesticides in North Santander. I think we have the bones of a deal. When one considers the security threat, and the continuing difficulties with wage settlements, the argument to settle this one quickly becomes difficult to refute. We should be willing to make this the last year that we use OP pesticides in North Santander. We should continue to minimize such use and remain open to alternative technologies. This approach will enable us to proceed with most (but not all) of the plans we have for expansion and replanting. It has been agreed that some of the high-altitude virgin sites, already secured for coffee, will not be cleared unless or until a cost-effective means of controlling red spider mite can be identified. The mites breed far more prolifically the higher you go. For its part, CBC will consider explicitly endorsing CS coffee from North Santander as bird-friendly. This is not guaranteed, but CBC will give it active consideration. I would hazard the chances of success at 60%, or maybe only 40% if there was extensive crop damage—CBC members are pretty canny operators. Both parties should jointly sponsor a bird survey to establish the evidence base. I think this is a very good deal and would commend it to the CS National Committee. The issues for CS, therefore, would seem to be whether CBC delivers on the brand support and the extent to which these new arrangements lead to mite damage next year. We know that the use of sprays will keep the damage down to 15% at maximum. Ideally, this will be below 10%, and I'm told that there's a 70% chance of securing such levels. Factoring in the considerably reduced acreage that this plan entails, CS could expect profits of $80m if the damage was minimal, reducing to $65m with significant (15%) damage. On top of that, CBC support would be worth about $10m next year.

Option E—Fair Trade Certification

During my negotiations with CBC and CS, I was put in touch with a Prof. Mannucci, an entomologist at the University of Pisa. He is anxious to deploy a field team to trial a predator-based control system for the red spider mite. Cost, however, is an issue. This would be a large-scale operation, with no guarantee of success. The predator concerned is a native lady beetle (ladybug) from Nicaragua. Associated risks include lady beetle infestation beyond the plantations and so environmental cordoning would be required—again, expensive. Prof. Mannucci needs at least 1000 hectares to make this worthwhile. The positive side of this is that CBC is prepared to fund most of the expedition costs. We are now examining the possibility of using a crew from the Geographic Channel to film the work which, if it comes off, would easily bridge the cost gap. This would be a gamble both for CBC (which would be sinking $500,000 into it) and for CS as it may yet lose coffee to the red spider mite. The possible gains may well be worth the effort though. Ms. Perez agreed to look at co-branded coffee, which could have huge commercial potential; and the university is proposing a three-way gain-share deal should the new technology prove a success. I think this may be worth a try.

Profit-wise, I've done some very broad-brush modeling. The Mannucci trials, by the way, are not entirely experimental, and there are sufficient lady beetle stocks in hand to treat coffee plants across the entire North Santander region if we so choose. Published peer-group research suggests that there's a 60% chance of the lady beetles confining crop damage to less than 10%. This would imply total profit from all estates at some $100m for next year. The same article suggested a 20% chance of damage between 11 and 20%, which would reduce profits to about $80m. At 20–30% (worst case, as there is an upper limit to mite damage) profits would fall to $70m. There is a 20% chance of such damage levels—representing a clear failure of the Mannucci's system under local conditions. Alongside these figures we need to consider the other benefits of the plan. Co-branded coffee, were it to become a reality, would generate an estimated $30m in any case. Perhaps more speculatively, profit sharing in Prof. Mannucci's new pest technology could be worth $20m a year. If the plan were a success, there would be a good chance (probably 60%) of both co-branding and profit-sharing; possibly a 15% chance of either benefit happening and only a 10% chance of no benefit materializing. If the experiment failed, CS would not get any profit share from Prof. Mannucci's scheme but might still secure a co-branding deal with CBC—say a 20% outside chance. Similarly, in the middle range of damage (11–20% crop damage) co-branding would become more practical, say a 60% chance.

All in all, this is a risky but fascinating proposition.

Initial Impact on Reputation

Another Action Research workshop for CS managers, led by the indefatigable Rodriguez, produces the following hypothetical media responses, which reveal much about the company's inner culture and priorities.

Option A—Only Spray a Little OP

Swallow Dive—New CS Brand Flops under Ornithological Blast

Sales of the new "Life's Little Luxuries" Colombian coffee brand have been highly disappointing. CS CEO Javier Rigas insists that the figures quoted are only preliminary and that the new marketing campaign has not yet completed its run, but it is not looking good for CS's latest move onto the supermarket shelves. The trouble concerns birds. The Campaign for Bird Free Coffee (CBC) ran a huge advertising blitz in North America and Europe with a scathing attack on CS's continued use of OP sprays. Snr. Rivas denied that the CBC campaign had impacted on sales.

Option B—Abandon OP Sprays

Breakaway Coffee Growers Form Rival to CS

Caffeine Supply, one of the world's largest coffee growers' organizations, was in turmoil last night after it was announced that a breakaway group of farmers had the support of over 20% of its members. Speaking for the new "Real Colombian" growers group, Pablo Marquez said that his members had had enough: "Friday was the last straw when Bogota told us that we could not use OP insecticides on our newly-cleared land. For many of us, that simply means paying to grow coffee, rather than earning a living from it. This is crazy." *Real Colombian* will sell its coffee wholesale on the world market in direct competition with CS.

Option C—Engage with CBC and TDS

Everything on the Table, Says Mediator

A round-table conference on the future of coffee growing in North Santander is to be convened in Bogota. Industry mediator Kenny Raval told reporters that he had persuaded all parties to attend the talks, in an attempt to address the deep-seated problems of the area. The immediate trigger to the crisis was a dispute between the Campaign for Bird Friendly Coffee (CBC) and CS over the use of pesticides. But Mr. Raval made it clear that he wanted to deal with pricing, wages and security, in an attempt to salvage an industry that has been on the slide for decades. The talks will convene after the current harvest, in three months.

Option D—Settle Quickly—OP Phase-out

Caffeine Supply Loses Ground but Gains Friends

The long-standing row between coffee producers and environmentalists in North Santander appears to have been resolved, at least for the current year. At a joint press conference, Christine Perez of CBC told reporters that her group "fully endorsed CS's environmentally sustainable coffee." This is a long way from the all-out boycott of *High Blue* coffee the group called for in Brazil. But CS has had to pay the price: it will stop using OP pesticides completely from next year and, even now, has agreed not to cultivate 18% of its newly acquired plantations in order to protect birdlife.

Option E—Fair Trade Certification

Beetlemania!

An Italian-led team of scientists is to spend a year in the mountains of North Santander, pitting Nicaraguan lady beetles against Colombian red spider mites. It's deadly serious for CS and CBC. They have teamed up with the Geography Channel to sponsor the world's largest biological coffee pest control program. If it works, they hope to eliminate the use of pesticides on Santander's estates and to promote a jointly branded "Bird Friendly Blend." Profit-share from the enterprise will include local education and development projects. Everyone in the area is rooting for the foreign lady beetles because Colombia's native red spider mites have been the scourge of its highland coffee crops for far too long. Maybe their time is up. These developments place CS in a strong position to apply for Fair Trade certification in its push to be recognized as a premium eco-friendly brand.

You agree with Master Facilitator Rodriguez that it is becoming clear which set of decisions will best help CS reach its objectives and satisfy all of its stakeholders. Together, you run a follow-up workshop designed to focus on media reaction and reputation.

Later Impact on Reputation—Media Reaction

Option A—Only Spray a Little OP

CS's decision to continue with limited organophosphate (OP) spraying for the current season has prompted barely a ripple in the Colombian press. Internationally, the dispute was picked up online, particularly by environmental groups and their sympathizers. These groups have been critical, probably responding to the Campaign for Bird Friendly Coffee (CBC) boycott. But overall, this has been a low-key event.

Option B—Abandon OP Sprays

There was some coverage in Bogota of the decision by CS to subsidize its North Santander operation in order to appease CBC, the group of campaigners for bird-friendly coffee. Appeasement was very much the tone of the articles, both on TV and in the print media. Oscar Falcones, owner of a huge coffee estate in Amazonias, claimed the industry faced bankruptcy "in order to save a few birds." CBC's views received scant coverage, although the initiative was picked up by BBC and others internationally. It is hard to view this as a PR win for CS.

Option C—Engage with CBC and TDS

The decision by CBC to enter into negotiations with CS rated a line or two in most of the national dailies in Bogota, with more extended coverage in the regional press. Locally it has been hailed as a victory for common sense, allowing as it does for the current year's crop to be gathered without hindrance.

Option D—Settle Quickly—OP Phase-out

Media interest in the deal recently secured between CS and CBC in North Santander was limited to a national TV interview, in which Christine Perez of CBC offered plenty of support for CS's efforts. This had little impact in Colombia, but there was a marked uptick in retail sales (5% per week in the US) when the interview went viral across "green" Internet sites, particularly in California. Ms. Perez's engaging personality and catchphrase "birds mean business" must have helped.

Option E—Fair Trade Certification

The landmark deal in Santander was a slow burner in media terms, but it really took off following the screening of "Andean Brinkmanship," an Australian TV documentary. A crew had followed the bird-care group's Christine Perez and CS Regional Coordinator Francisco Villa for a week as they hammered out the deal. It made riveting viewing. Since then the jointly branded "Bird Sense" coffee has hit the shelves, and the duo has been inundated with calls. Early sales have been phenomenal around the world. Interest may well continue into next year, as a team headed by Prof. Mannucci, an entomologist at the University of Pisa, completes its work—also with a camera crew in tow.

Meanwhile, CS fully expects to be able to place the Fair Trade mark on its labels very soon. This is expected to enhance the brand's image as socially responsible as well as eco-friendly.

Taking the "Action Research" work (Plan—Act—Observe—Reflect and then plan again) initiated by you and Fernando Rodriguez[1] to the ultimate, CS CEO Javier Rigas wants managers to work their way through quantitative assessments of each Pentalemma option.

General Impact on Firm Value

Option A—Only Spray a Little OP

Controlled Spraying

COMPANY REPUTATION: Continued use of the OP sprays brought a boycott from the CBC against CS products. This was not received well by investors or local producers. The red spider mite needs to be exterminated if we are to hit our expected yields for the year. Fortunately, only a small number of our producers use the more dangerous OP spray, so the overall impact in the future may not be so high. All said and done, this equates to a net value of negative $5,000,000.

SALES: Sales were down amid the boycott and the fact that CS cannot label its coffee as organic. There are plans for future expansion, but without a solution to the insecticide/red spider mite problem, this could be in jeopardy. In total, the net value added was only $4,000,000.

RISK MANAGEMENT: FARC activity in the region is up, apparently in response to the return of the death squads. The spiral of violence may be with us again, although it is too soon to draw that conclusion. But security costs have climbed. Another risk is that of lost production if wet weather continues to exacerbate the red spider mite problem. The net value of these risks is negative $2,000,000.

SAVINGS IN SUPPLY COSTS: With decreased sales and production, CS was unable to gain from its normal economies of scale. In addition, shippers were concerned that we might spread the red spider mite problem across the region and demanded a premium on our shipments—to cover the cost of extra inspections, they said. All told, we were only able to save 40% of our original expected savings. This led to a net value of $3,500,000.

STAFF MOTIVATION: Staff motivation, all the way from head office to plantation supervisors and laborers, is lower since the upsurge in violence, and especially since the murder of a local union activist. Oddly, the vocal CBC campaign and boycott seem to have had less impact on the workforce. However, in a nation with climbing unemployment, most locals are still happy just to have jobs at the moment. This situation could turn at any time, but for now, it remains positive with a net value of $1,500,000.

Option B—Abandon OP Sprays

Scale Back

COMPANY REPUTATION: CS's decision to scale back production in the worst-infested red spider mite locations proved to be the right solution to the pesticide problem. CBC is no longer threatening a boycott on our products, and local farmers understand the impact that CBC's last campaign had against our Brazilian competitor *High Blue*. The decision led to a positive net value of $1,500,000.

SALES: Sales remained level. We decreased production in the seriously infested areas, and these happen to be those with the lowest yield; so that many ill effects were avoided. Our increased production and new plantation areas made up for this decline on the southern farms. The resignation of several farmers to form a break-away producers' group came too late to impact heavily on this year's figures. Sales estimated net value is $5,000,000.

RISK MANAGEMENT: The main risk other than a product boycott was FARC violence, especially in the southern areas. The security situation was sensitive. A "no contact" order with the paramilitary groups was enacted and seemed to lessen some of the tension. Although our decision concerning the sprays has cost money, it has certainly reduced many business risks. Net value added is $2,500,000.

SAVINGS IN SUPPLY COSTS: Supply cost savings were not secured this year, as farmers contended with the contraction in land under coffee and increased fuel costs. There was no net value added for supply cost savings under this option.

STAFF MOTIVATION: Staff motivation has been at a reasonable level under the circumstances. Removing production from the southern areas helped to ensure that the FARC elements operating there would leave our workers alone. There remains concern about the death squads that have been popping up around the country. We value staff motivation at $1,500,000 for the year.

Option C—Engage with CBC and TDS

Dialogue

COMPANY REPUTATION: Bringing together all the parties involved was the right move for CS to make in terms of reputation. CS was able to get CBC to back down from its current demands by iterating what effect a boycott would have on the local economy and workers in the region—CBC doesn't want bad press either. This was also good for the share price when investors saw that talks were taking place to help rectify the situation. The net value is $4,000,000.

SALES: With over 3,500 hectares in production and more to come, production was up and so were sales. The FARC threat remains, but has had no impact on our volumes. Overall, this accounted for a net value of $9,000,000.

RISK MANAGEMENT: FARC remains the biggest threat to the region. Although it did not worsen through the year, this does not mean that we are out of the danger zone yet. The para-military group still operates with impunity in many areas of the country where we produce coffee. Although the talks with CBC and others have for now mitigated a lot of commercial and reputational risk, security costs remain high. Risk management is currently valued at $2,000,000.

SAVINGS IN SUPPLY COSTS: Higher production means lower supply costs due to economies of scale and increased purchasing power. CS was able to meet targets set forth at the beginning of the year. We expect these savings to continue. The net value of these savings for the year is $3,500,000.

STAFF MOTIVATION: Staff motivation remains good for the moment. The biggest concern was the risk imposed by the FARC forces. Fortunately, we did not see any attacks on our workers or production facilities this year. We can safely say this added $3,000,000 in net value.

Option D—Settle Quickly—OP Phase-out

Winning CBC Support

COMPANY REPUTATION: CBC is happy that our company will not use OP pesticides after this year, a full two years ahead of the government deadline. This played well with the media and boosted CS's reputation generally. The jointly sponsored bird survey and the association of CBC with our brand helped this along as well. The overall net value added to the company's reputation is $5,000,000.

SALES: Sales were robust on the back of strong production figures. CS was able to kill off the red spider mite population using the

OP chemicals at specified marginal sites where mite infestations were worst. Accordingly, production levels estimated at the beginning of the year were on target. The net value of this is $10,500,000.

RISK MANAGEMENT: The risk that CBC would boycott CS product was reversed to the extent that CBC now endorses CS coffee as bird-friendly. Security problems and costs persist, but there can be little incentive for our local workers to become involved with violent groups so that we are hoping such threats will recede. The net value of mitigating the environmental risks with the CBC is estimated to be $3,000,000.

SAVINGS IN SUPPLY COSTS: There were minimal supply cost savings this year, in range with projections made in last year's budgeting forecasts. The higher use of newer GM pesticides (as opposed to the cheaper OP ones) had its impact here. These savings amounted to $5,000,000 in net value.

STAFF MOTIVATION: Staff morale has been good this year, with a surprising degree of interest in the new deal. Growers in marginal areas were relieved at being able to continue using the OP sprays for another year, until a more tenable solution can be found or the red spider mite infestation decreases. For our staff, nervousness about security persists, but attendance and sickness levels are good. The net value is $3,750,000.

Option E—Fair Trade Certification

Co-Branding and Biological Mite Control

COMPANY REPUTATION: In allowing a more environment-friendly method to combat red spider mite infestations, CBC and CS entered into a co-branding arrangement. This proved to be the correct choice. Also, Geographic Channel's documentary helped to improve CS's image across the world. As news spread, share prices increased based on the improved relationships. The estimated net value is $7,500,000.

SALES: Sales were as projected—the lady beetle project worked well, and the crops could be harvested with minimal losses attributable to the red spider mite. Also, the increased publicity of the documentary and the co-branding of the coffee led to a surge in demand for our product worldwide. The estimated net value added to sales was $16,000,000.

RISK MANAGEMENT: The biggest risk was that the predatory lady beetle experiment would not work and we would have to continue using OP sprays, to the detriment of our image. Alongside continuing security costs, we beefed up our coffee futures portfolio as insurance against crop failures. Risk protection measures this year, however, have decreased against last year. This approach led to a net value of $4,500,000.

SAVINGS IN SUPPLY COSTS: CS was able to meet projections and keep its supply chain costs low and within the predicted range. Most savings accrued from not having to pay for insecticides. Therefore, there was a net value of $4,500,000.

STAFF MOTIVATION: Staff have been tremendously supportive of the partnership with CBC. Most were able to see the long-term potential of the deal and that enhances their future security. We have seen improved productivity and reduced sickness this year. The estimated net value of this option is $4,250,000.

Reflecting on Chapter Two

The Scenario in Context

The situation described in this scenario required consultants to focus on a difficult technical and environmental problem associated with pesticide use. The backdrop was again North Santander, with the assumption that the industrial relations dispute described in Chapter One had been resolved—at least for the time being. This part of the country remained unstable however, with increasing levels of violence. A large employer such as CS needed to be mindful of such circumstances and to avoid strategies that might heighten this risk.

The chief antagonist for this scenario was CBC—the Campaign for Bird-friendly Coffee. CS had a good starting point from which to engage with CBC, in that its basic farming technique protected the forest canopy and hence the birds. Unfortunately, the insect problem, at its worst in those marginal areas CS was hoping to open up to new production, implied chemical spraying. CBC was implacably opposed to the continued use of organo-phosphate sprays.

Dilemmas and Challenges

An early challenge for managers here was to come to grips with the technological options, their strengths and weaknesses. There were actually four approaches built into the various options presented, in different ways: (a) abstain from spraying, (b) use OP sprays, (c) use species-specific sprays or (d) employ predator-based controls. None of these "solutions" was quite as simple or straightforward as might have been imagined, and the strategies available to the teams often featured the use of more than one technology. Throw into the mix the other factors, such as the television sponsorship deal available with Professor Mannucci, or the pressure from Bogota concerning the national growth plan, and the situation becomes quite a tangle.

Various means of providing some clarity were available to managers. In particular, the "Action Research" method (Plan—Act—Observe—Reflect and then do the same with a revised plan) as explained and demonstrated by Fernando Rodriguez would have been highly appreciated.

The other major dynamic in this situation was the relationship with CBC. The fact that the two organizations had enjoyed a constructive relationship in the past obviously suggested some scope for resolution, although it was equally clear that the question of OP pesticides was a fundamental one for CBC. Careful judgments were required as to the value of potential support (or of outright hostility) from this influential environmental lobbyist. The threat of a product boycott—as had already been implemented in the neighboring country, Brazil—was real. It might have been worth risking a boycott in order to safeguard the vital expansion plan. Or, was there a means of squaring this triangle through compromise?

Background factors, such as the risk of violence also influenced potential outcomes. Would a withdrawal from the marginal areas be of benefit on security grounds? Managers were seriously challenged by this range of competing risks and opportunities.

Note

1. For the past 15 years, Fernando Rodriguez has trained management professionals in the latest tools and techniques, building for himself a reputation for helping companies develop lasting improvements. His approach begins with building a consensus on the definition of the problem to be solved. From there, he employs several methods of gathering ideas, such as brainstorming and mind-mapping, and then harvesting potential solutions by using an affinity diagram or similar tool. In short, Rodriguez works with managers to clarify their goals, and agree on the changes they need to make to achieve them. In his words, "I simply help managers become dynamic agents of change themselves.

Further Reading

Elkington, J. (2002). *Cannibals with forks: the triple bottom line of 21st-century business.* Oxford: Capstone.

Freeman, R. E., Harrison, J. S., & Wicks, A. C. (2007). *Managing for stakeholders: survival, reputation, and success.* New Haven, CT: Yale Univ. Press.

Galtung, J. (2012). *Peace by peaceful means peace and conflict, development and civilization.* Oslo: Prio.

Kahane, A. (2012). Transformative scenario planning working together to change the future. San Francisco, CA: Berrett-Koehler.

Nelson, J. (2000). *The business of peace: the private sector as a partner in conflict prevention and resolution.* London: International Alert.

Chapter Three

Force Field Analysis

For a third year, you are on assignment representing Pentalemma Inc. in the North Santander region of Colombia, advising plantation operator and coffee producer Caffeine Supply. Having worked its way through the transition from pesticides to biocontrol in battling the destructive red spider mite, the company now faces accusations that coffee plantations are to blame for recent deadly floods. A new local mayor heads this barrage and is demanding action. At the same time, the CS expansion plans are again thrown into doubt as it faces the challenge of tribal politics with respect to a newly acquired tract of land. The signing of a major new supermarket deal with a company in the USA ratchets up the pressure to increase production. Meanwhile, there are signs that FARC rebels are recruiting disaffected workers and tribespeople.

You and your Pentalemma colleagues need to understand the multi-faceted series of challenges facing CS CEO Javier Rigas and his management team. These interrelated challenges seem to pull CS in a number of different directions.

On your desk is an update from CS Regional Coordinator Francisco Villa.

From: Francisco Villa, Regional Coordinator, Norte de Santander
Subject: Flooding and expansion plans

The election of Pablo Sanchez as mayor here in Cucuta last month has changed the complexion of negotiations concerning any future expansion of coffee production. By way of background, Sanchez campaigned for the Movimiento Campesino (Peasants Party) on a radical ticket promising to address the flooding of the Rio Molesto.

For two years now, the river has burst its banks during the rainy season, causing widespread disruption to subsistence farming and the transportation infrastructure. It also caused great inconvenience to many lowland dwellers. From a strictly selfish perspective, the floods are not such an issue for our producers: We farm on upland mountainsides, and these drainage problems effectively hit most of our farms "downhill." They have been blamed as well for the catastrophic cholera epidemic of two years back. Cholera and malaria remain rife here and are related to the drainage situation in the lowlands. During the peak of the epidemic, the farmers lost 20% of their workforce. We would want to avoid a repeat of that.

There seems to be little doubt that the floods are the result of exceptional rainfall—you will recall that this in itself has been a problem for coffee production. Unfortunately, however, CS's local expansion plan, which has seen approximately 500 hectares of new coffee production in North Santander over the past three years, is being blamed. There is no evidence for this whatsoever. But critics suggest that the felling of trees, necessitated by turning mountain jungle into coffee plantations, is exacerbating the drainage problems. We might want to commission some work on this. We need to bear in mind, and indeed I stress this myself, that we retain the largest trees as top cover for our coffee plants. These are the ones with the extensive root systems that protect against flood damage.

The Mayor has a skilled assistant in former TV journalist Elena Garcia. She is termed the "Flood Tsarina" in these parts. We need some support nationally to contest these allegations—or find ways to work with the Mayor's office in a more constructive manner. The Mayor's current proposal is to pay for flood defenses via a turnover-based tax on business.

This issue coincides with some existing tensions concerning the purchase of additional land. I refer to the village of Taganga, where

CS (myself as the lead negotiator) has agreed to pay $300,000 for 35 hectares of ideal coffee land upon which the village sits. These people (the Awa) are villagers with a tribal culture. Most are anxious to embrace a more modern and prosperous existence. The village held a plebiscite and voted to accept the deal. Most of the people will move into modern units in Cucuta, built by CS; many will have jobs working with our farmers. All would be well but for an occupation organized by Manuel Tenorio, the 20-year-old son of the village chief. Tenorio and his supporters wish to maintain a "traditional" tribal lifestyle of hunting and gathering. In fact, the Awa tribe no longer fish in the way they used to, and sadly, this seems to be a culture in decline. The community is also shrinking fast in terms of raw numbers.

There is a worrying security angle to all of this. Since last December's FARC offensive in North Santander, sporadic violence has been commonplace. I am told that local support for the guerrillas has rocketed because the going rate for plantation work fell. You will recall that the recent world coffee price crash meant we had to drop our day rates back to $3. Now I am told that there are "discussions" between FARC and the young men who are occupying the village.

We need to secure this land in order to continue our development plan; it would be useful to have the support of the Mayor in this, but instead, we find ourselves embroiled in a silly argument about floods for which we are not responsible. The situation in North Santander is therefore highly volatile at present.

Francisco Villa
Regional Coordinator

You start your analysis work in discussions with the Pentalemma team.

The flooding issue may feel a little unfair, in that it is not at all certain that CS's high altitude coffee plantations have anything much to do with the problem. The Mayor has turned this into a highly charged local political issue. Blameless or not, CS cannot afford to ignore it. With the arrival of the UN Food Agency, which is interested in flood protection for the lowland farmers, CS at least has the prospect of a more impartial player on the scene.

The tribal issue presents a rather different kind of local politics. Keep in mind that the villagers concerned are in fact split. A solid majority voted for the CS purchase plan. The fact that the protestors are actually occupying the site, and that there is talk of an alliance with FARC, means that simply driving through the deal by fiat would be risky.

There seems to be a security "perfect storm" developing: a decline in effective government control of the outlying areas, an increase in FARC activity and recent wage cuts on the plantations leading to FARC recruitment of disaffected workers. At the same time, the US supermarket deal means growing long-term demand. Therefore CS badly needs those new acres.

Your team is therefore presented with a complex setting in which to advise on a strategy for CS. There will be several themes to develop for consideration by the client:

1. The importance of political pragmatism.
2. Tribal cultures and tribal politics.
3. The risk of commercial over-stretch.

The many issues raised in the scenario include flood hazards; disease epidemics; special business taxes; loss of government control and the challenge of a de facto guerilla "shadow government."

Scenario Design

Two major themes combine in this scenario, with the intention of posing a challenging "trilemma" and illustrating how it can sometimes be possible to reconcile diverse problems through one broad strategy. If they choose the right option, managers will find not only that they successfully tackle the twin issues of the villagers and the flooding, but that in doing so they protect business growth and mitigate the security risk.

The first aspect of the "trilemma" is the flood question, looked at in ethical and practical terms. If we take it that the Mayor's claims about the causes of the flooding are wrong, does that mean that companies like CS should refuse to participate in possible solutions? The practical advantages in acceding to the Mayor might be overall benefits to the community, combined with a better rapport with his Administration; but at the expense of conceding an invalid point and, probably, hard cash.

With the villagers, subtle questions about the inherent value of traditional cultures might arise, even if the majority in the community concerned vote for "modernity." The angry young men camped out at the village may just have a point about the importance of their culture, as well as posing a threat to delay and frustrate development. Managers will find that there is actually some middle ground here, and that solutions exist which serve both to address the concerns of the radicals and to protect the heart of the development plan.

The central point in the scenario is one about elegant, broadly drawn solutions that can address a multitude of risks. It would be wrong to pretend that such openings always arise, but they will never do so where business remains introspective. Key concepts for managers aiming for a triple bottom line (people, planet and profit) include a determination to actively search for more creative solutions and in doing so, to ensure that all relevant stakeholders are included in that process. Analysts and managers that maintain that agility without getting hung up on details such as the villagers' vote or the veracity of the Mayor's claims will be more likely to succeed.

Questions to Consider

1. Which should come first: a big new sales contract or the capacity to deliver it?
2. Is there a value to be placed on indigenous cultures beyond the democratically expressed wishes of the community concerned?

3. Is there a distinction between political pragmatism and immoral conduct? How should businesses draw the line here?

Significant risks in Chapter Three include:

Legal: The new Mayor of Cucuta, Pablo Sanchez, threats to hike local business taxes up to 20% in order to pay for flood protection. CS could be seriously disadvantaged by such a decision.

Environmental: Exceptional rainfall has been the main cause of flooding in North Santander, and it has been a problem for coffee production in the area.

Social: CS could provide new jobs in Cucuta for individuals from the Awa tribe, along with a more modern and prosperous lifestyle. This scenario, however, could accelerate the decline of the Awa population.

Economic: Due to the recent world price crash, the rates for coffee have dropped, potentially decreasing the company's profits dramatically. CS has lowered its daily wages for plantation workers to $3.

Political: CS's local expansion plan is being blamed for the flooding in North Santander. CS needs to have the support of the local community in order for its business to remain profitable.

Following a vigorous exchange of views with your team and his own managers, Regional Coordinator Francisco Villa pens a pair of possible options, neither of which appears entirely palatable.

Option A—Discredit the Mayor

This situation may not be as concerning for CS as it seems. To take the floodwater dispute first, the evidence rather stacks up on CS's side, and the new Mayor has a low standing with CS's allies in Bogota. Accordingly, this issue can be handled through the media. We should use our influence to portray Sanchez as Colombia's version of Chavez (an unbalanced maverick). The danger is retaliation by way of a big flood tax this year—and we have to accept that there is an 80% chance of this transpiring.

We should also make a serious case that canopy farming protects against soil erosion. If CS throws its weight behind the UN flood initiative, it may also secure some sympathy for the problem at the village of Taganga. This one is tricky. But the key point is that we have a group of young hotheads defying the democratically expressed wishes of the rest of their community. Unfortunately, chances are that CS's new project at Taganga will be delayed by the protestors this year, if not stopped altogether; but we cannot simply capitulate to this kind of blackmail. My local journalist contact pitches the likelihood of the project being completely frustrated as high as 50%, with a 40% chance that it will simply be delayed for a month. CS should insist that the authorities deal with this—but not by knocking heads together. If we nip this in the bud, we should avoid the risk of further FARC involvement.

Without a special tax and with a smooth project at Taganga, we can expect profits to come in at $100m for the year. Unfortunately, we estimate that an emergency flood tax would cost a whopping $50m. These are high stakes. A delay of a month at Taganga would halve profits. It is far trickier to calculate what might transpire if the project were blocked altogether for a year, but our best estimates project profits of only $25m should that occur, or $10m following a Mayor's tax.

Option B—Avoid Over-extension

The range of risks now facing CS in North Santander is such that it may be wise to secure the current level of coffee production, rather than rest the company's national strategy on further expansion. This would it seems, preclude the new deal with US supermarkets—over-extension has been the undoing of many a large multinational corporations (MNCs). CS should consolidate its current position and think in terms of further market expansion only when it can be sure to bring higher production.

Of course, this cautious approach entails the sacrifice of some future profit and does not entirely eliminate existing risks. The Mayor's threatened flood taxes will definitely impact on CS, so a plan is needed for tackling them financially. Although there may only be a one-in-five possibility of the full 20% tax on turnover, that possibility needs to be assessed. More likely is the 10% tax, with a 70% probability, according to my source in the Mayor's office. The much talked of "one-off windfall tax" is looking less likely now—a one-in-ten probability.

The Mayor's colorful assistant is all over the local news, threatening a new law to hold coffee growers to account for soil erosion; they could be fined. This would be in addition to the flood taxes. Some political legwork is required down there before this becomes a reality. Working alongside the UN flood program may be the price to pay—but certainly, CS should abandon plans for more coffee hectares this year. This would take the sting out of the Taganga dispute as well. In any case, CS must avoid antagonizing FARC. I fear this is the reality and that our talks will be characterized by the need to deliver a difficult message.

Another risk faced by CS in this situation is that some of the farmers will break away to form a rival cartel. The establishment of the *Real Colombian* group was threatened before. It has to be acknowledged that this becomes a strong 60% possibility should CS retrench in this way. This does not invalidate such a stance, but it would cost an estimated 25% of all net profits for the year.

Optimum bottom-line projections for the year would be at $40m with this strategy of retrenchment. However, that assumes only a "one-off" flood tax. The 10% tax would cost an additional $10m and the 20% tax another $10m on top of that. Any breakaway cartel would lose CS a further 25%, as cited above. So these numbers cover quite a span. Yet they do take full account of the reduced amount of land envisaged, and importantly, CS would effectively be mitigating future risk at the price of a more modest current year.

Force Field Model

With Option A and B in hand, you seek approval from CEO Javier Rigas for a half-day workshop involving your team and all available CS managers. When you explain that you intend to utilize a management tool called Force Field Analysis, a technique with which he is familiar, Rigas quickly agrees and frees up the CS North Santander calendar.

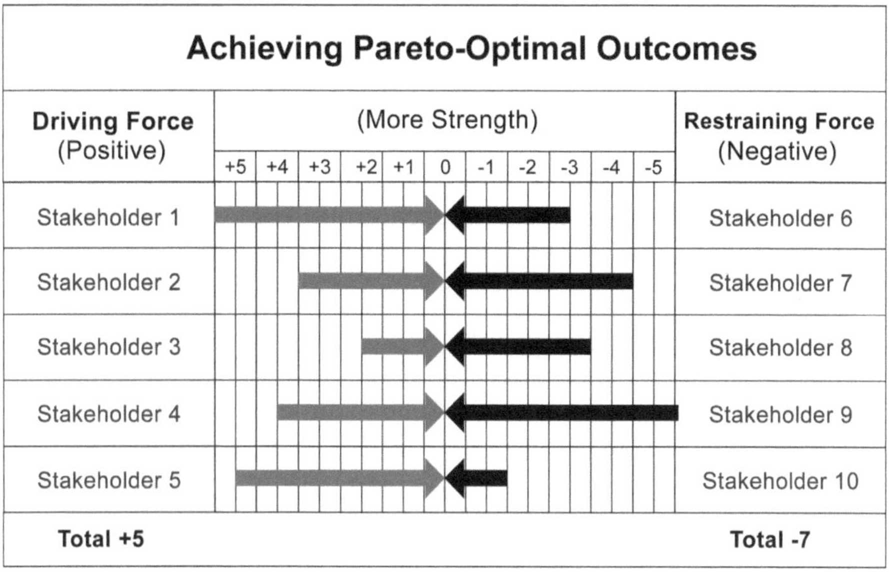

Figure 3.1: Kurt Lewin's 1951 Force-Field Analysis applied to stakeholders.

In Kurt Lewin's force field analysis (see Figure 3.1 here below), there are forces that support or resist certain goals to varying degrees. If one's objective is to change something in an organization, it can be useful to know in advance how much support and resistance to expect in order to prepare accordingly. One way of completing a force field analysis is to ask whether the roles that specific stakeholders play are supportive or resistant toward certain goals. In general, corporate stakeholders fall into one of three groups; those motivated more by environmental goals, those motivated more by social goals and those motivated more by financial goals (Elkington, 2002). The disagreements or issues between stakeholders are often rooted in these different motivations. Once the stakeholders are grouped in this way, their basic issues of disagreement become easier to identify and resolve. After confirming the stakeholder groups, their interests and the issues between them, a force field analysis can be used to prioritize the issues so they can be addressed one by one in the order of urgency and importance.

Besides Rigas, however, few CS managers are familiar with this management tool. On the day of the workshop, they seem eager to learn about and apply it. There are some spirited arguments amid constructive discussion. Bit by bit, a visual summary emerges of the various factors influencing the North Santander situation for CS and its stakeholders. Even so, opinions vary on how to quantify each of the forces and how to interpret the overall graphic. You invite the participants to form three groups, and each group comes up with its own additional option for consideration in the final analysis.

Option C—Slow Down and Talk

Our priority down in Cucuta should be to attempt to defuse the situation at the village. Taganga has the potential to turn quite nasty, given reports concerning FARC and the reputation of the Colombian police. We should meet the dissident villagers and attempt to establish a dialogue. "Jaw jaw is better than war war," as Churchill said. The chances are that if we approach this in a civilized manner, we will ultimately be able to develop the site at the village. But the diplomacy will cause a delay, with a 50% chance that this impacts on CS's bottom line for the year.

Heated debate concerning flooding could also benefit from the volume being turned down. We already have a meeting scheduled with the Mayor's assistant Ms. Garcia. The purpose of this is to establish a factual basis for further discussions. What exactly is the evidence linking soil erosion from the high-altitude coffee plantations and these floods? Independent research should provide the answer. The politics are difficult, however. Even with dialogue with the Mayor's office, there is a 50% chance of a 10% tax on turnover being introduced this year. There is even talk of a 20% tax, with a 20% likelihood of that. There is also a 20% possibility of a one-off payment, and even a remote chance that there will be no charge on business for anti-flood work this year.

Profits will be affected accordingly. With no flood tax, they are estimated at $100m. A one-off payment would reduce this to $80m. A 10% tax would leave CS with a net profit of only $50m in Santander, whilst the suggested 20% tax would leave $40m. Against these figures, a significant delay to the village project would halve any net profit.

It really is too soon to say what options might be open to the various parties in order to secure progress here. It seems certain, though, that some sober reflection at a slower pace would be of benefit to all.

Option D—Full Cooperation

It probably is not wise for CS to attempt to sit on the high moral ground with respect to the flooding issue in North Santander. The evidence does not really support the allegations made by the Mayor's office, but it would be worth paying a price to secure help from that direction in connection with Taganga. Better perhaps to offer full co-operation and support to the promised UN flood relief scheme. If there are practical measures that the UN team (who must be regarded as objective) would recommend to CS's farmers, then these should be looked at positively. It looks certain that the Mayor will levy some kind of charge on industry to contribute to the flood protection work. This could be a one-off payment or a tax on turnover, rumored to be at 10% or even 20%.

The villagers at Taganga are a trickier proposition because of the binary nature of the dispute. Is there a compromise possible here? Simply offering to raise the price would appear crude and is likely to backfire. A close examination of the protestors' "manifesto"—they have posted it online—proved worthwhile. A key concern is the ancestors' burial ground, a holy site for the Awa people. Yet this is on the edge of the proposed acquisition and probably covers less than half a hectare. Another consideration is the forest itself. CS has done fantastic work with CBC on forest management in North Santander. The cost of losing the burial ground alone would be negligible. If CS had to lose (say) the equivalent of 50 more hectares of production, this would cost about $10m in reduced profits for next year. But I believe there must be a 60% chance of striking a deal based solely on the burial ground.

Overall profit for the year would, therefore, depend mainly on the Mayor's flood tax. A one-off payment, for which there is only a one-in-ten chance, would leave net profits of $160m. The likeliest bet (60% chance) is a 10% turnover tax. This would reduce profits to $100m. The other alternative is a 20% tax, which would cost a further $20m. From all of these figures, one would need to deduct the cost of losing those

50 hectares—should that transpire. There is surely room for dialogue and compromise, if needed, bringing CBC to the table. If all parties are prepared to be flexible, this multifaceted problem can be peacefully resolved.

Option E—Community Benefit

A careful study of the Awa people, with input from an anthropologist in Bogota, form the backdrop to much of this proposal. We also have data from the Colombia Hydrological Survey, also in Bogota. The result is an idea to canalize or even dam the River Molesto upstream of Taganga. Geologically and hydrologically, this may well be feasible, subject to survey, costings and other studies. The appeal to the faction in Taganga that wishes to retain a traditional lifestyle would be the establishment of mountain fisheries, replacing those lost during the 1970s and 1980s due to logging. Whilst preserving the burial ground at Taganga (entirely feasible), it would be possible to offer a new village site, possibly lakeside, within three miles. The coffee planters would have a secure water supply for the dry season, and there may even be some scope for hydroelectric power. If so, this should be used for community benefit. At the lower levels of the province, this would more than offset any possible flood risk associated with the coffee plantations. It would avoid the need for much of the flood protection work envisaged by the UN Food Agency—and the possibility of diverting the funding toward such a project should be actively pursued. In that case, there should be no question of paying tax to build flood defenses. However, there may well be an argument for CS investing in the dam project. The UN is already looking at such a possibility. A provisional survey has identified three possible sites. The likeliest (with a 60% probability of selection) is to the north (Site A); it promises significant hydroelectric power (HEP), but would cost CS a lot of hectares. In the center, Site B (30% chance) would be a middling option. Probably the best from CS's perspective is site C, to the south. This would not produce HEP though—its chances are rated at only 10%. On a brighter note, there is a 70% chance that the UN and the Colombian government will fund the entire project. Failing that, CS would pick up about $30m of costs in year one.

If this scheme goes ahead—it is almost shovel-ready due to modular building techniques and the relatively small scale—it may well be completed within a year. Early costings for CS take into account cheap HEP for plant and accommodation and huge transport savings with the construction of a new road up the valley. As such, profits are pitched at $130m, $180m and $130m for Sites A, B and C, respectively, exclusive of any construction costs falling to CS.

CS should examine this scheme for feasibility. If it passes muster, then it could provide the platform for a sustainable and harmonious future for the area. In acting as a catalyst for such a project, CS could be seen to give something back without spending more than a reasonable amount.

At this point, let us fast-forward to consider five hypothetical sets of consequences.

Initial Impact on Reputation—Media Response

Option A—Discredit the Mayor—Villagers "A Bunch of Hotheads"

The North Santander representative for CS has dubbed the Awa tribal protesters at Taganga "a bunch of hotheads." Snr. Francisco Villa made the remarks in a TV interview for Cucuta Tonight in which he also called for the forces of law and order to remove the protesters. But the Mayor's office seemed unmoved. Spokeswoman Elena Garcia said that it was "about time CS faced up to its social and environmental responsibilities."

Option B—Avoid Over-extension—Mallmart Walks Away from CS Deal

Mallmart CEO Steve Simmons made it clear last night that the supermarket giant was not interested in a deal of any sort with CS. "If these people cannot deliver against production undertakings, Mallmart cannot work with them," he said in a short statement. CS's shares were already on the slide this week in reaction to the decision to abandon a major new plantation following a protest by indigenous local villagers. There will be worried faces in Bogota when dealings begin again on Monday; the rumors in Phoenix were that the Mallmart-CS deal could have been worth more than $100m.

Option C—Slow Down and Talk—Flood Tsarina in Fighting Mood

Ms. Elena Garcia, the colorful assistant to the new Mayor of Cucuta, has promised a "robust exchange" when she meets representatives of CS next week. The Mayor's office accuses CS's farmers of contributing to the flash flood problem which has become an annual feature of Santander's weather. Ms Garcia has even threatened to introduce punitive local legislation to deal with what she calls the "coffee problem." Others are more sanguine. CS limited itself to a statement indicating that it was glad to be talking to the Mayor's office about a problem "we all share."

Option D—Full Cooperation—Mayor Sanchez Welcomes Business and UN to Cucuta

The long-heralded talks between the Mayor, Pablo Sanchez and the UN flood advisory team kicked off in earnest yesterday. Already, the Mayor and his team have drawn support from the local business community. Plans have not yet been formulated for the barrages and dams that, it is hoped, will spare the low-lying countryside from annual flooding, but a fund has now been established. The "Voluntary Flood Levy" on business will be an annual voluntary payment, invited from those businesses that employ over 20 people and based on turnover. FIAT Colombia and CS have each committed $500,000 a year, and the fund now stands at $3m.

Option E—Community Benefit—High Dam Plan Attracts New Employers to Santander

Now that the complex joint funding structure has been approved for the High Dam project in North Santander, firms from around the world are beginning to eye the Cucuta region for possible investment. "Safeguarding what had been the flood plain will be fundamental," explained Mayor Sanchez. "We will have cheap land for light manufacture and cheap energy as well." But the Mayor has been clear that any benefits must be shared with the community. "Just as Caffeine Supply has been sympathetic to local need up in the mountains, we will take the same line on the plains." He means it: The vegetable canning company, Vegrite, has secured one of the first construction licenses, but only after having promised to build workers housing and a school.

Later Impact on Reputation—Media Response

Option A—Discredit the Mayor

CS's strategy in Santander has become conflated with a broader political row between Cucuta and Bogota. As such, CS has been portrayed as in cahoots with the President. More sophisticated analysis (BBC, for example) also addresses the shortcomings of Cucuta Mayor Sanchez. Government mouthpieces have of course depicted him as Hugo Chavez Mark II. None of this is good for CS's reputation; shares have dipped (4% this month) as foreign investors fight shy of pumping in fresh funds. Being portrayed as the enemy of environmental protection is not a good place to be in. Fortunately, the situation at Taganga has not made national news as yet.

Option B—Avoid Over-extension

The decision not to proceed with the Taganga site made good television, as the 20-year-old son of the Taganga village chief, Manuel Tenorio, and his followers paraded triumphantly in traditional Awa costume. But, nonetheless, it reflected well on CS as did the limited coverage that accompanied Snr. Villa's meeting with the "Flood Tsarina." At least CS was seen to be talking.

Option C—Slow Down and Talk

Coverage of CS's work in respect of the flood problem and land acquisition at Taganga village has been muted. It has featured both Elena Garcia at the Mayor's office and Mr. Tenorio at the village "talking a good fight," with CS necessarily taking a more conciliatory tone. This has played well.

Option D—Full Cooperation

Sometimes the media finds a good news story less exciting than a bad one. The coverage of the Taganga deal was limited to the local TV news. Taganga village chief Manuel Tenorio did a lot of handshaking, which was positive. CS's involvement with the Mayor's team and the forthcoming UN flood work did get a wider showing—all positive.

Option E—Community Benefit

Reaction to the Molesto dam scheme has been positive throughout. The icing on the cake was the big splash in the Latin American edition of Newsweek Online, which included impressive "what if" graphics. On the back of this, CS has been assailed by hundreds of investment queries. This not only pushed the shares up (13% on the month), but also opened the prospect of a new share issue.

General Impact on Firm Value

Option A—Defying the Mayor and the Protestors

COMPANY REPUTATION: Due to our contacts within the local media, CS's reputation remains relatively sound. The company's methods of clearing forests for coffee production are seen to be done in an environmentally safe manner. What could not be prevented were the protesters outside of our proposed Taganga development site, which did not play so well. There were also some press allegations that CS had been conspiring with the national government, but these gained little traction. Altogether, there was a positive net value of $1,000,000.

SALES: Although sales remained steady, the recent drop in coffee prices has damaged the bottom line of the company. With the expansion to Taganga still up in the air, we may not be able to increase production as much as we had hoped. The net sales value is $4,000,000.

RISK MANAGEMENT: The flood tax cost us this year and will continue to do so until the local political scene changes. Another threat is that some workers are turning to the FARC militia. This is because we had to cut wages back to $3 per day when the bottom fell out of the coffee market. The net value of all this is estimated to be a negative $5,500,000.

SAVINGS IN SUPPLY COSTS: Supply costs were up with the recent flooding in the area as many of our main transport routes were disrupted. This cost the company and made it difficult to get our supplies out to our distributors. In the end, this amounted to a net value of negative $1,750,000.

STAFF MOTIVATION: Staff motivation has been mixed. On the one hand, the wage decreases sent some of our workers running to the FARC. On the other, most workers are glad to have a job that pays them anything at all. The assessed effect on net value was, therefore, zero.

Option B—Consolidation Rather than Expansion

COMPANY REPUTATION: Despite our decision to scale back development plans, the Mayoralty has chosen to portray CS as the primary cause of recent flooding. This was unfortunate, given the high-profile meeting between the Mayor's office and CS on this matter at the beginning of February. CS's co-operation with the UN team has done little to mitigate this either. The only silver lining was the de-escalation of the Taganga dispute, now on the way to resolution in light of the decision to reduce hectarage. But this strategy has done little to address a huge threat to the standing of CS: its perceived culpability in repeated local flooding. The net value of this is estimated to be a negative $1,000,000.

SALES: Sales have stagnated for the year, especially since the US supermarket deal could not be closed. Without expansion to Taganga, although demand exists in the USA, CS simply would not have the capacity to meet it in the long-term. The impact of this was a modest $5,000,000 sales value.

RISK MANAGEMENT: The one-off tax that was imposed may not be a one-off after all. There are also real issues concerned with fines for soil erosion, but the local authorities are so far unable to attribute that directly to the coffee growers. With development frozen and further large costs hanging over the company, the risk landscape has been dire. The estimated net value of these risks is negative $2,500,000.

SAVINGS IN SUPPLY COSTS: Flooding in the region has completely disrupted our logistics. Our supply chain is suffering unnecessarily (and by our own doing if the "Tsarina" is to be believed) and the only hope that we have is that the rainfall will ease and the local environment return to normal. We estimate these costs to have a negative net value of $1,750,000.

STAFF MOTIVATION: Some of the farmers are threatening to form a cartel, which means that their morale is low at the moment. CS lost three producers (it could have been much worse). In contrast, the workforce has been largely contented over the past 12 months. The total net value of staff motivation is $1,250,000.

Option C—Slow Down and Talk—Diplomatic Measures

COMPANY REPUTATION: Diplomacy went a long way in securing the reputation of CS in North Santander. The company was able to proceed with the acquisition of the Tanganga village area although it took longer than expected. Unfortunately, all of the flooding in the area has investors worried about the reliability of the region's supply, and the stock price has been depressed. In total, the net value of this is $2,000,000.

SALES: Sales increased with the addition of the 300 hectares to CS's productive farmland. Thankfully flooding in the area has subsided and the company was able to get its coffee to distributors for sale. The new 10-year deal that has just been struck with a large supermarket chain is good news for all involved. The total sales net effect is $8,000,000.

RISK MANAGEMENT: A positive engagement with all parties has gone some way to reduce the likelihood of punitive taxes and to safeguard the CS Development Plan as well. Other risks concern FARC and security. The delays implied by the diplomatic approach have done little to address those risks. On balance, therefore, a slightly improved risk environment for the current year. This is valued at $1,250,000.

SAVINGS IN SUPPLY COSTS: Flooding in the area was relatively minor for the year. This is good news for us, our distributors and the logistics MNC that we have a long-term deal with. We are also able to use the MNC's purchasing power to get lower shipping costs. The net value for our supply chain network was $1,500,000.

STAFF MOTIVATION: Staff have continued to work productively through the year, with acceptable attendance, productivity and sickness levels. There have been no strikes or walkouts. The decision to engage constructively with the Mayor's office has probably offset the potential for trade union involvement in the thorny issue of flooding (The Mayor's political party has some close ties with the TDS). This is worth an estimated $2,500,000 in net value to CS.

Option D—Cooperation on the Flooding Issue

COMPANY REPUTATION: CS offered its full support to the UN flood team in the area even though we believed our own activity was not a major factor. By letting the Taganga members keep their tribal burial ground, we were able to avoid any potential backlash. The net value of the company's reputation is $3,000,000.

SALES: Sales increased as the Taganga land moved into production. Coupled with the new long-term deal for coffee sales to a US supermarket chain, the outlook is promising for the next several years. This has a positive effect of $11,250,000.

RISK MANAGEMENT: The risk register for CS in this part of Colombia demonstrates a fair degree of control, despite the major uncertainties apparent at the start of the year. We now have the flood politics effectively neutralized, with an annual payment of $500,000. This avoided the need to make another major provision in next year's accounts—we had set aside $2m for the current year. $500,000 we can live with. Similarly, the Taganga deal means we are now able to plan: no costly security teams to worry about. This turnaround is worth a net value of $3,000,000.

SAVINGS IN SUPPLY COSTS: Supply cost savings were bolstered by the new long-term agreement with the US MNC. Economies of scale and the ability to tap into their international shipping infrastructure has saved an estimated $2,750,000.

STAFF MOTIVATION: The villagers in the newly acquired Taganga are happy about their burial grounds remaining untouched. Across all local staff and growers, CS's involvement with the UN shows that they care about the local community and are not simply extracting a profit from them and their homeland. Staff morale has been buoyant: this resulted in a net value of $3,500,000.

Option E—Community Benefit—Molesto Dam Project

COMPANY REPUTATION: The Company enjoyed a boost in its reputation for improving the living standards of the Awa people in the Taganga region. Even the "Tsarina" herself could not argue this point. Improved goodwill for improving their village and leaving the burial site in place both benefitted the reputation of CS. We estimate this to be an additional net value of $5,500,000.

SALES: This project, although heavy in terms of capital outlay, has already secured major sales dividends. Our new US contract is fully activated, and we have the hectares, transport and stability to comfortably meet its requirements. Our product lines have seen something of a surge in demand, as word spread globally about our plans for the Taganga village. CS estimates the net value of this to be $15,500,000.

RISK MANAGEMENT: The dam mitigated future flood risks. The chance that the Awa people might side with FARC militants is very low now that we have restored clean water and fishing sites that they have not enjoyed in nearly 30 years. Insurance premiums are down, alongside security costs. This equates to a net value of $4,500,000.

SAVINGS IN SUPPLY COSTS: A new road that came with building the dam increased the savings for CS in the region. The supply chain was improved and benefited the locals, a real win-win situation for all involved. Extraction costs were lowered with the HEP dam although it cost CS some hectares. Estimates of net value are $3,000,000.

STAFF MOTIVATION: Restored fishing reservoirs, hydroelectric power and clean water went a long way to bolstering the motivation of the workforce. There has been a palpable sense that CS has done the right thing here—and this has translated into excellent industrial relations. We calculate that the net value of this decision was worth upwards of $6,000,000 in staff motivation.

Reflecting on Chapter Three

The Scenario in Context

Having coped with industrial unrest and the dilemma of pesticides versus the environment, in this last Colombian scenario, managers were presented with a completely different environmental challenge, coupled with a new twist on the continuing project to expand coffee production in the region. The environmental issue concerned a spate of recent floods which, although mostly affecting lowland farmers (i.e., not coffee producers), were being blamed on CS. A local Mayor was proposing a tax on turnover to fund flood defenses. At the same time, plans to open up more land were in danger of being thwarted by a group of radical tribal villagers.

Dilemmas and Challenges

This was certainly one of Pentalemma's more "political" scenarios, focusing as it did both on the politicization of the flooding issue and the split within the Taganga villagers. The overarching challenge was to identify strategies that might span these issues and hopefully address some of the background risks as well. The contention written into this situation—between the moral and the practical made it difficult to reach agreement. Such disagreement often surfaces when politics intrudes, underlining the need for effective teamwork. Importantly, with both "political" arguments used here, there was a need to look behind the more obvious positions being taken. In this sense, they required a counter-intuitive approach.

The Mayor's position concerning the floods contained more than a hint of downright dishonesty. This might have been "accommodated"—by accepting his case and stepping up to support the anti-flood measures—or challenged. The scenario made it difficult to determine which might be the most cost-effective way forward before considering the moral ambiguities. On this latter point, there was also the more straightforward notion of philanthropy—social investment for its own sake.

Similar dynamics applied in the case of the villagers, where a conventional democratic outlook would suggest supporting the majority view. The protestors at the site were a minority of young radicals, arguably clothing themselves for convenience as defenders of traditional culture. But it seemed that their peers were more interested in progress.

The situation set up here was, therefore, a matrix of moral and practical political problems, with the lurking challenges of the FARC guerrillas and the newly struck US supermarket deal serving as a backdrop. Should CS surrender to the Mayor's view on flooding, recognizing that even if it doesn't, he might tax them anyway? What about the protestors at the village, with their shady links to FARC? Are halfway positions in any way tenable and if so, are they morally valid? Perhaps CS should concede one of the two arguments, but contest the other? These are the dilemmas that the Pentalemma and CS teams faced. The need to find broader solutions—to link these problems together and adopt a coordinated response—posed a greater challenge.

Further Reading

Elkington, J. (2002). *Cannibals with forks: the triple bottom line of 21st-century business.* Oxford: Capstone.

Freeman, R. E., Harrison, J. S., & Wicks, A. C. (2007). *Managing for stakeholders: survival, reputation, and success.* New Haven, CT: Yale Univ. Press.

Galtung, J. (2012). *Peace by peaceful means peace and conflict, development and civilization.* Oslo: Prio.

Kahane, A. (2012). *Transformative scenario planning working together to change the future.* San Francisco, CA: Berrett-Koehler.

Nelson, J. (2000). *The business of peace: the private sector as a partner in conflict prevention and resolution.* London: International Alert.

Conclusion

Highlights of Chapter One

Some of the more important themes that this scenario was designed to highlight are considered below. Note, however, that this list is not exhaustive.

Several of the options presented to the managers included creative suggestions for greater staff involvement in the future of the business. Option C, for example, brought them into the thinking behind the new marketing strategy. Such an approach will tend to improve motivation and lessen the likelihood of industrial action. This is not quite the same thing, however, as sharing both risks and benefits with the workforce. In a situation where there are major areas of mutual interest, this can make sense for both parties. The ideas of profit share and fair trade both imply that there may be bad times as well as good. To the degree that must remain appropriate and equitable, workers actually take on some of the company's risk—and benefit directly when the company does well. Options D and E both included this concept, with good outcomes for motivation as a consequence. It was Option E, with its broader commitment to a longer-term and more imaginative new deal for the workforce, which secured the best all-round result in this scenario.

A company's risk costs will relate strongly to the security situation in a tense area such as Colombia. Where those tensions are high, it is clear that costs such as insurance premiums will rise. Less obvious but nonetheless demonstrated by several studies, is the link between the security climate and the overall social and employment situation in an area. An employer such as CS can make a big difference in a case such as this, where its commodity is such a major part of the local economy. Reading through the options, managers will have seen that the risk of violence and instability goes up if less attention is paid to the conditions offered to the workforce. So that although Option A may hold a superficial appeal in terms of protecting investment and revenue, those who chose it will have seen that it triggered not only a strike, but an increase in FARC violence. The benefits accruing from risk management took a major dip. Such changes may also have been evident in the volatility gauge. To the extent that the other options address this question, the payoffs and reports—particularly in the area of risk management—reflect this tendency.

One of the tensions common to much modern management is that between the short and long term. It would seem folly to sacrifice the important strategy agreed for the North Santander region on the altar of a short term pay deal. This is exactly what Option B proposed, with consequent dips in production and sales. Although there is no simple answer to this dilemma, a balanced approach is likely to prove the wisest. Option E safeguarded investment by avoiding a commitment to an immediate pay hike whilst advocating a much fairer system of reward and involvement. In contrast, Option A protected the investment, but at the cost of a breakdown in industrial relations.

Highlights of Chapter Two

In Chapter Two, some of the more important themes that this scenario was designed to highlight are considered below, in the context of the options which were available to managers.

The co-branding option, with its three-way partnership deal, was the most imaginative one available to managers. The outcomes for CS included greatly increased sales, a much-improved company reputation and buoyant staff morale. Breadth was the key here—Professor Mannucci's plan stepped outside the zero-sum game of pesticide versus environment and introduced lucrative sponsorship opportunities as well. Co-branding with CBC would very obviously generate a market boost for CS. The possibility of profit-sharing, should Mannucci's new technique prove effective, could add to that. In return, CS is facilitating the piloting of the lady beetle project on a large scale, largely financed by television rights.

This kind of win-win solution becomes much easier to identify where a company views other organizations and interests within its environment as potential partners. Restructuring local institutions can also help to bring different perspectives and interests, new resources, and complementary knowledge and skills. A genuine openness to partnership work should be part of every manager's toolkit—particularly when dealing with environmental issues: our global environment is a project we all have an interest in.

This scenario illustrated the manner in which technologies can generate as many problems as they solve, implying a need for a careful analysis of the situation from all angles. OP pesticides are cheap—and still legal during the period in which this scenario was set. Looked at one-dimensionally, a decision to proceed with controlled OP spraying may have made sense; but the undoubted benefits of controlling the spider mites by this means would have been countered by a product boycott and sales slump. On the other hand, the "pull back" choice—effectively abandoning the expansion plan, would have led to lower sales and greater supply costs. While Prof. Mannucci's bold initiative represented the optimum outcome, other choices, such as that of reduced spraying, envisaged a mixed approach. It is the knock-on impact of technology that can take business by surprise—i.e., not what it was designed to do, but its side effects. Such issues bring their own costs and risks.

Whether the decision was to bring CBC into the debate after the harvest, negotiate a reduced spraying regime or take the bold Mannucci plan, there were plenty of choices here that recognized the value of engaging with vocal critics of the business. All of these options turned an opponent into an ally, with varying benefits for CS in areas such as sales and reputation. It is rarely the case that confrontation leads to a better business outcome.

Highlights of Chapter Three

One of the less obvious but nonetheless important features of this scenario was the pressure placed on the managers because of the new US supermarket deal. There is a lesson here about overreach, in that big commitments such as this can be premature if a company does not have reliable means in place to meet them. In this scenario, though, it is effectively too late: the supermarket contract is a fact that must be dealt with. The consolidation and retrenchment option will sabotage it, at great cost, as well as leading to the establishment of a rival coffee-growers consortium.

The depiction of the Awa tribe in this scenario was researched and based on historical events (albeit not involving the real Awa people). Companies caught in the middle of such arguments can feel that they can't win whichever option they choose, and however well disposed toward local culture and tradition they might be. Unless a really creative solution can be found, such as the dam project, the best approach is to attempt to find a compromise and work for goodwill on both sides. Politics within traditional cultures can resemble its more "modern" counterparts, or take on sometimes surprising dynamics. In a volatile region such as North Santander, a decision to ignore one side is likely to be a mistake. The "defiance" choice in this scenario resulted in risk costs escalating, as predictably enough, support for FARC in the area grew. Simply assuming the local authorities will deal with such a situation because it is their job to do so can be naive and dangerous.

CS needed to swallow some pride in this scenario and work practically with the Mayor, taking some assurance that the UN, also interested in the flood problem, might provide objective support. Although the scenario is careful not to spell out definitively that the floods are not due to coffee growing techniques, this is heavily implied. Nonetheless, the floods are a real and very serious problem for this region. Even if CS is blameless, there is a good chance that business is going to be asked to share the cost of solving the problem; and in any case, it should regard itself as a part of this community. At the very least, a dialogue is called for with the UN and the Mayor, in recognition of these circumstances. At best, managers will have spotted the significant benefits of the dam scheme, which is the optimum strategy to adopt in this scenario. It represents full engagement with the problems of the region, and it is one of the company's own employees who unearths the possibility of this project.

The kind of capital outlay that such a scheme can mean for a company will often be weighty, but the end result can pay dividends across all areas. The opening of the new road, for example, leads to big supply cost savings for CS. Local politicians have real responsibility and real power. Where they have the clear backing of the community, it is folly indeed to refuse to engage in debate about such an important question, whatever may have been said during the cut and thrust of an election campaign.

Other Books by this Author

Multi-Hazard Disaster in Japan

Learn about disaster management following an earthquake in Kyushu. By advising Brighter Brand Japan, a company with retailers around the country, you acquire logical thinking skills, and the ability to distinguish between long-term strategies and short-term tactics.

Conflict Minerals in the Democratic Republic of Congo

In the Democratic Republic of Congo, you advise Speedy Devices, one of the world's largest consumer electronics producers. You will acquire a range of risk management tools as you help your client resolve complex issues related to profit, child labor and the role of business in a conflict situation.

Mining Conflict in the Philippines

Welcome to Mindanao, an island in the south of the Philippines. You will help Massive Metals, a foreign mining company, to manage its stakeholders. You will learn to use problem-solving tools to resolve environmental and political issues.

Notes to Self

Chapter One

1. Who are the main stakeholders?

2. What are the stakeholders' main interests?

3. Which issues do the stakeholders disagree about?

4. Which of the above issues is the most critical one?

5. If the most critical issue is not resolved, what might happen to the stakeholders and your client?

6. Which option do you think is the best one for your client to choose?

7. How will the different stakeholders benefit from choosing the option you suggest?

Chapter Two

1. Who are the main stakeholders?

2. What are the stakeholders' main interests?

3. Which issues do the stakeholders disagree about?

4. Which of the above issues is the most critical one?

5. If the most critical issue is not resolved, what might happen to the stakeholders and your client?

6. Which option do you think is the best one for your client to choose?

7. How will the different stakeholders benefit from choosing the option you suggest?

Chapter Three

1. Who are the main stakeholders?

2. What are the stakeholders' main interests?

3. Which issues do the stakeholders disagree about?

4. Which of the above issues is the most critical one?

5. If the most critical issue is not resolved, what might happen to the stakeholders and your client?

6. Which option do you think is the best one for your client to choose?

7. How will the different stakeholders benefit from choosing the option you suggest?